General Science

AGS

7/8 RR
H21

by
Sally Ann Cooper, M.S.
Carolyn Cradler, M.S.
Michael Spurrier, B.E.S.

W9-AMV-445

AGS®

American Guidance Service, Inc.
4201 Woodland Road
Circle Pines, MN 55014-1796
1-800-328-2560

Experiences in Science

Printed in the United States of America

ISBN 0–7854–0970–X (Previously ISBN 0–88671–710–8)

Order Number: 90891

A 0 9 8 7 6 5 4

Contents

Unit 4: How Living Things Work: Introduction to Biological Processes

• Investigate 1—*The Earth Is a Puzzle* •

Scientists think the top solid part of the earth, the lithosphere, is broken into a number of large pieces called *plates*. These plates are constantly in motion, with some plates moving into one another, while others are separating. In this investigation, you will construct a map made out of the plates. Then you will identify some of the features on the plates.

Materials
map of the plates (page 6)   paste
colored pencils   scissors
2 sheets of paper   globe or world map

Procedure
1. Carefully trace the plate pieces and the land areas on them on page 6.
2. Cut out the pieces that you traced.
3. Arrange the pieces into a map of the earth just as you would a jigsaw puzzle.
4. Paste your map onto a separate sheet of paper. Be careful to make the edges of the pieces match.
5. Label the following countries, continents, and oceans. Use a globe or map to help you if necessary.
   a. Africa   e. Europe   h. Atlantic Ocean
   b. United States   f. North America   i. Indian Ocean
   c. Asia   g. South America   j. Pacific Ocean
   d. Australia

Observations
1. On which plate is most of the continental United States located?

_____

2. On which plate is the southwestern part of California located?

_____

3. The place where the two plates in answers #1 and #2 meet is called the *San Andreas Fault.* Why do you think many earthquakes occur there?

_____

4. Notice that part of Asia is on the Indo-Australian plate. What country is located on its northwestern tip?

_____

5. This separate part of Asia is moving northwest into the rest of Asia. The Himalayan Mountains are located where these two plates meet. How do you think these mountains were formed?

_____

 Investigate Further

The plates have been in motion for millions of years. To see how the earth may have appeared 225 million years ago, look up information on Pangaea, the supercontinent made up of all the earth's continents, in reference books or on the World Wide Web.

• Investigate 2—*Where the Earth Quakes* •

Earthquakes are one of the most destructive forces on the earth. They occur when parts of the earth's lithosphere suddenly move. Scientists who study earthquakes have found that earthquakes are much more likely to occur in some areas than others. In this investigation, you will locate on a map some earthquake-prone areas. Then you will compare these results with the map of the plates prepared in the previous activity.

Materials

world map on page 9   Data Table 1
completed plate map   pencil

Procedure

1. Table 1 lists the latitudes and longitudes of 18 locations where major earthquakes have occurred in the past.

2. Look at the map on page 9. Find the latitude and longitude for each location and mark it with its letter. For example, you will mark an *A* at 45° S and 70° W, a *B* at 40° S and 180°, and so on.

3. When you have completed locating each earthquake area, you are ready to answer the questions in Observations.

Data Table 1		
Earthquake	**Latitude**	**Longitude**
A	45° S	70° W
B	40° S	180°
C	20° S	70° W
D	5° S	140° E
E	5° N	80° W
F	10° N	75° W
G	15° N	90° W
H	20° N	100° W
I	30° N	85° E
J	35° N	50° E
K	40° N	120° W
L	40° N	140° E
M	45° N	15° E
N	50° N	145° E
O	55° N	180°
P	60° N	145° W
Q	65° N	130° E
R	65° N	15° W

Observations
1. Around which ocean do most earthquakes occur?

_____

2. Along which coast of North America do most earthquakes occur?

_____

3. Which state in the United States is the most earthquake-prone?

_____

4. Compare your map of earthquake locations with the map you assembled of the lithosphere's plates. On what parts of the plates do most earthquakes occur?

_____

5. The boundary between the eastern North American plate and the western Eurasian plate is mostly beneath the Atlantic Ocean. The island of Iceland is one place where this boundary is above sea level. What is the latitude and longitude of Iceland?

_____

6. You learned in the previous investigation that the plates are slowly moving. How does this fact help explain why most earthquakes occur where they do?

_____

_____

_____

Investigate Further
The energy released by an earthquake is measured on the Richter scale. The Richter scale uses numbers to indicate how strong an earthquake is.
1. Find out what the strongest earthquakes measured and where they were located.
2. How strong were the biggest earthquakes that occurred in the United States?

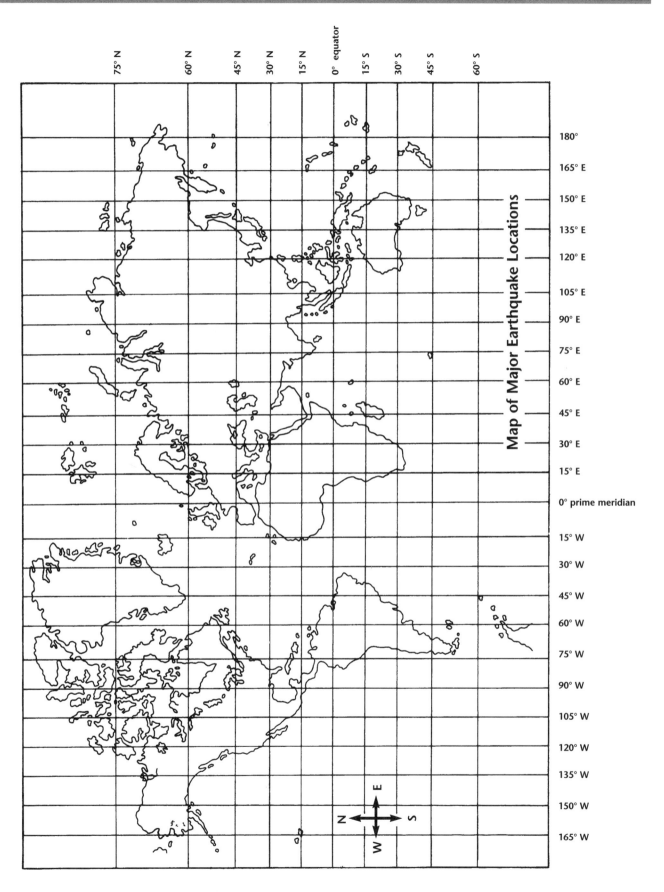

Map of Major Earthquake Locations

• Investigate 3—Inside the Earth •

It is about 6,400 kilometers (4,000 miles) to the center of the earth. The deepest holes that have been drilled into the earth's surface are only about 9.7 kilometers (6 miles) deep. Most of what is known about the deeper parts of the earth has been learned indirectly. For example, you can learn about the earth's interior by studying the patterns of earthquake waves as they travel through the earth. Scientists have learned in this way that the inside of the earth is layered. In this investigation, you will use a hard-boiled egg as a model to study the inside of the earth.

Materials
hard-boiled egg
pencil

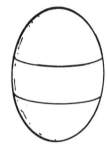

Procedure

1. Each person or pair of lab partners will need one section of hard-boiled egg prepared by your teacher.
2. You will use the egg slice as a model of the inside of the earth.
3. In the box on this page, draw a picture of the inside of the egg slice. Include all three layers. If your yolk is off to one side, draw it centered in your diagram.
4. Label the layers you drew:
   a. the shell   *the Crust*
   b. the egg white   *the Mantle*
   c. the yolk   *the Core*

Drawing of a Model of the Inside of the Earth

Observations

1. Look at your egg slice-earth model. Which layer of the earth is the thinnest?

   _____

2. What layer is found under the crust?

   _____

3. As you go deeper into the earth, the temperature continually gets hotter. Which layer would have the highest temperatures?

   _____

4. Since you cannot cut through the real earth in this way, which is the only layer you are able to study directly?

   _____

5. The shell of your egg probably cracked when your teacher cut it. In what way is the real earth's crust like the cracked eggshell?

   _____

   _____

   _____

Investigate Further

Each layer of the earth has different features. Look up information about the three main layers of the earth in a reference book or on the World Wide Web. You will want to find out about the material in each layer, its temperature, and how each layer affects the earth as a whole.

• Investigate 4—*Getting to Know Minerals* •

Minerals are solid substances formed naturally in the earth. There are about 3,000 different minerals that scientists have described and named. Different minerals are identified by their physical properties such as color, luster, and shape. Color is helpful in identifying a mineral, but, unfortunately, some minerals come in more than one color. The ability of a mineral to reflect light is called *luster.* If the mineral is shiny like a metal, it is called *metallic.* Minerals that do not have luster are called *dull.*

Texture describes how a mineral feels. *Streak* is the color of the powdered line left when a mineral is rubbed against a piece of unglazed tile. Very hard minerals will only scratch the tile and not leave a streak. The *hardness* of a mineral is measured by how difficult it is to scratch. Each mineral is given a number from 1 to 10, going from softest to hardest. Sometimes one mineral is used to scratch another. Some minerals are *magnetic.* They will attract steel and iron particles.

In this investigation, you will perform six tests that are used by scientists to identify minerals.

Materials

6 different minerals, A–F	unglazed piece of tile
steel butter knife	glass microscope slide
penny	loose staples

Caution: Handle the knife carefully when scratching a mineral with it.

Procedure

1. Look carefully at mineral *A.* Record its color in the data table on page 14.
2. Next, notice if the mineral is shiny or can reflect light. Record in the data table the luster of your mineral.
3. Feel your mineral. Is it smooth? Is it rough? Does it feel slippery or greasy? Record the type of texture your mineral has in the data table.
4. Rub your mineral against a piece of tile. If it makes a streak, record the color of the streak in the data table. If it does not leave a mark, write in the table "No streak."
5. First, try to scratch your mineral with your fingernail. If it scratches, your mineral is a #1 or #2. (See the following chart.) If your fingernail will not scratch the mineral, try to scratch it by using the penny. If the penny does not scratch it, go on to the next test until you have scratched the mineral. (A mark that wipes off is not a scratch!) Record the number in your data table.

Hardness Number	Test for Hardness
1	Fingernail scratches it easily.
2	Fingernail barely scratches it.
3	Penny leaves a scratch mark.
4	Steel knife scratches it easily.
5	Steel knife barely scratches it.
6	Mineral scratches glass easily.
7	Mineral scratches steel easily.
8	Mineral scratches other minerals.
9	Other minerals cannot scratch it.
10*	The hardest mineral.

Unless your mineral is a diamond, you will not get a #10.

6. See if the loose staples are attracted to your mineral. If they stick to it, your mineral is magnetic. Write *yes* or *no* in your data table under the "Magnet" column.

7. Now repeat these six tests on the five remaining minerals. Record your results in the data table.

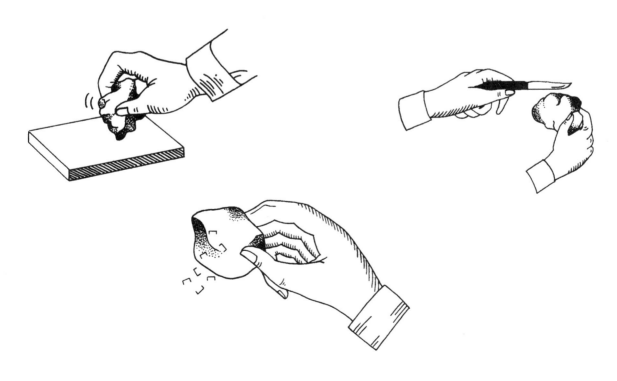

Mineral Identification Data Table						
Mineral	Color	Luster	Texture	Streak	Hardness	Magnet
A						
B						
C						
D						
E						
F						
Other						

Observations

1. Which mineral was the hardest?_____

2. Was the color of any of your minerals different from the color of the streak it made?

   If so, which ones? _____

   _____

3. Which, if any, minerals had metallic luster? _____

   _____

4. Were any of the minerals you tested magnetic? If so, which ones?_____

   _____

Summary

1. A mineral that attracts iron or steel is called _____.

2. _____ is measured by how difficult it is to scratch a mineral.

3. The shininess of a mineral is called _____.

4. The shade or hue of a mineral is called _____.

5. A mineral that is not shiny is called _____.

6. The powder mark left by a mineral is called a _____.

7. Minerals that shine like metal are called _____.

8. A _____ is a solid, naturally forming substance found in the earth.

9. _____ describes the way something feels to the touch.

Investigate Further

1. Using the information you collected on one of your minerals, try to identify the mineral in a book of minerals.
2. Test and try to identify other minerals that you might have in your home or school.
3. Go to a museum that has a mineral collection to see many more examples of minerals.
4. Learn about how some minerals are cut into gems for jewelry.

• Investigate 5—*Some Famous Rock Groups* •

If you look at the rocks you find outside, you will see that they come in many shapes and materials. Not only are rocks made of different minerals, but they are not all formed in the same way. In this three-part investigation, you will learn about how rocks in the three main rock groups are formed.

Part 1   Making Igneous Rocks

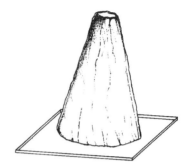

Materials
modeling clay   aluminum foil
pencil   baking soda
white vinegar   red food coloring

Procedure
1. Shape the clay into a "volcano" cone about 8 cm (3 inches) high.
2. Place your model volcano on a sheet of aluminum foil and press up the edges of the foil to form a tray.
3. Push the eraser end of your pencil into the top of the volcano to make a vent. The vent does not have to go all the way to the bottom.
4. Fill the vent with baking soda. Do not pack the baking soda in too tightly.
5. Mix a few drops of red food coloring into the vinegar. Stir until the vinegar turns completely red.
6. Slowly pour the colored vinegar into the vent.
7. Keep adding vinegar until all of the baking soda has reacted.

Observations
1. What happened when the vinegar was added to the baking soda? _____

_____

2. In what way is this like a real volcano erupting? _____

_____

3. What did you see happening to the sides of the volcano during the "eruption"?

_____

_____

4. Why do real volcanoes often grow larger after an eruption? _____

_____

5. The material that comes out of a real volcano is hot, melted rock. What do you think

happens to the melted rock? Tell one way that rocks form. _____

_____

Part 2   Making Sedimentary Rocks

Materials
magnifying glass   sand
clay particles (soil)   gravel
small, clean milk carton   plaster of paris
plastic spoon   water

Procedure
1. Look closely at a few particles of sand with the magnifying glass. Then look at a few particles of clay. How does the sand compare in size to the clay?
2. Next, compare the sand and clay with the gravel. The gravel is much larger. Do you think that they all could be made of similar material?
3. Cut or tear off the top of the clean, empty milk carton.
4. Add 3 spoonfuls of gravel to the bottom part of the carton.
5. Next, add 6 spoonfuls of sand and 2 spoonfuls of clay particles.
6. Add 6 spoonfuls of plaster of paris and mix well.
7. Slowly add water to the mixture, a little at a time. Stir the mixture until the plaster of paris is like thick whipped cream and the gravel, sand, and clay are coated with it.
8. Put your milk carton in a place where it will remain undisturbed overnight.
9. After the mixture has hardened overnight, tear away the milk carton. Study your new "rock" so you can answer the following questions.

Observations
1. Look at your model rock. Can you still see pieces of gravel in it? _____

2. Can you still see pieces of sand?_____

3. Can you still see pieces of clay? _____

4. What was added to the plaster of paris to stick all the particles together? _____

5. In nature, water that sinks into the ground can help glue together soil particles to form rocks. What name is given to these rocks? _____

Part 3   Making Metamorphic Rocks

Materials
modeling clay in several colors
waxed paper

Procedure
1. Take small pieces of clay and roll them into balls about the size of peas. You will need about 30 balls in a variety of colors.
2. Divide the balls into two equal piles and gently shape the piles into two large balls. Be careful not to change the shape of the little balls of clay. You have now made two models of sedimentary rocks.
3. Next, place one of the rock models between two pieces of waxed paper and press down on the clay with the palm of your hand. You should press hard enough so that the small clay balls change their shape.

Observations
1. Look at both the clay ball and the one that was flattened. How has the shape of the little balls changed in the flattened one? Draw a picture of the shapes of some of the changed clay balls.

2. In the flattened ball, are the colors of the little clay balls still separate, or are they becoming mixed together? _____

3. Rock that is changed by great pressure and heat is called *metamorphic rock*. *Metamorphosis* means "to change." Do you think that this is a good name for this kind of rock? Why or why not? _____

_____

Investigate Further

In this investigation, you have learned that there are three main ways in which rocks form. Rocks form when hot, melted rock material comes out of volcanoes and then cools and hardens. Another type of rock is made up of small pieces of gravel, sand, or clay that become stuck together with water and minerals. A third type of rock forms when other rocks are changed by great heat and pressure.

You have seen how sedimentary rocks can be changed into metamorphic rocks. It may surprise you to learn that if conditions are right, all types of rocks may change from one kind to another. This is called the *rock cycle.*

- Igneous rocks form whenever melted rock material cools.

- Sedimentary rocks form whenever other rocks are broken down into smaller pieces and the pieces are "glued" back together.

- Metamorphic rocks form when other rocks are changed by great heat and pressure.

1. On the diagram of the rock cycle, write the words *Cools, Broken Down,* or *Heat and Pressure* on each arrow to tell how one kind of rock can be changed into another.

2. Which type of rock would you call the "parent," or original, rock material? Why?

_____

_____

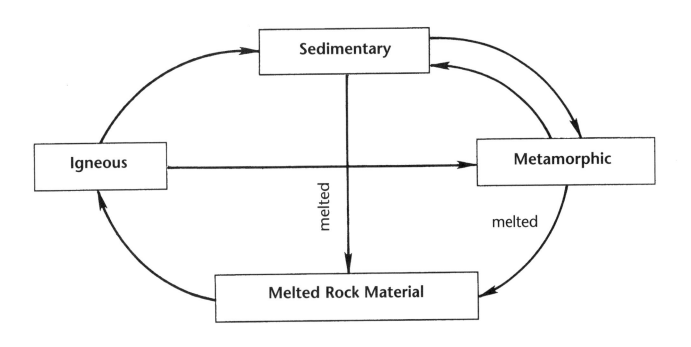

• Investigate 6—*Forces Behind the Winds* •

Did you know that it is really the energy from the sun that causes the winds to blow? Wind is just air in motion. In this investigation, you will discover how energy from light can cause air to move.

Materials
15-gallon aquarium
black construction paper
rubber tubing
smoke source (incense, punk, etc.)

200-watt light bulb in a lamp with a reflector
funnel
board to serve as a partial lid for the aquarium

Caution: Do not touch the light bulb or the burning smoke source. Allow the smoke source to burn out before you place it in a fireproof can and douse it with water.

Procedure
1. Set a lamp with a 200-watt bulb about 10 cm (4 inches) above one end of an aquarium.
2. Place a sheet of black construction paper directly beneath the light in the aquarium.
3. Attach a funnel to a piece of rubber tubing that is long enough to reach the bottom of the aquarium as shown in the diagram.
4. Place a board over the top of the aquarium so just an opening for the light remains.
5. Turn on the light for two minutes.
6. While the light is still on, your teacher will light the smoke source. Let the smoke travel up through the rubber tubing to the inside of the aquarium.
7. Observe the pattern that the smoke follows.

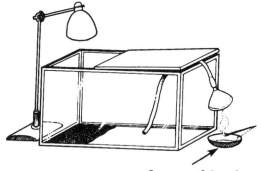

Source of Smoke

Observations
1. Draw in the diagram above the pattern the smoke followed. Use arrows to show the direction in which the smoke moved.
2. Watch the smoke. What does its movement tell you about the air inside the aquarium?

_____

_____

3. Watch the smoke as it moves near the piece of black construction paper. Does it move up or down? _____

4. What happens to the smoke as it reaches the top of the aquarium?

   _____

   _____

5. Can you think of a reason the black piece of construction paper was placed under the light?

   _____

   _____

   _____

6. Look at the picture below. Think of how the sun's light would cause the air to move over the warmed earth. Draw arrows on the picture to show the direction in which the air would move.

Investigate Further

   1. The winds move around the earth in broad bands called *belts.* Find out about the wind belts. Which wind belt do you live in?
   2. Because the earth is spinning on its axis, the wind patterns around the earth become curved. This is called the *Coriolis effect.* Research information on the Coriolis effect.
   3. In this investigation, you saw that heated air rises. What examples can you find in your kitchen, bathroom, or other places that demonstrate this fact?

In order for it to rain, clouds must form. Clouds, therefore, must contain the water that becomes rain. In this investigation, you are going to make clouds.

Materials

quart jar with lid	hot water
oven mitts	match
aluminum pie pan	ice

Caution: Use the oven mitts as you pour the hot water out of the jar. Stand back as your teacher lights the match and drops it into the jar.

Procedure

1. Fill the jar with hot water.
2. Put the cover on the jar and let it stand for two minutes.
3. Open the jar and pour out the hot water.
4. After your teacher drops a lighted match into the jar, quickly replace the lid.
5. Set an aluminum pie pan filled with ice on top of the jar.
6. Watch what happens inside the jar.

Observations

1. How did the inside of the jar appear after the match began to smoke and you chilled it with ice? _____

2. What was left in the jar after the hot water was poured out that helped form the cloud? _____

3. For a cloud to form, water vapor in the air must condense, or change to a liquid. How did the pan of ice help the cloud form? _____ _____

4. The smoke supplied small particles in the air on which the water vapor could become a liquid. What are some sources of particles in the air when real clouds form? _____ _____

Investigate Further

Different types of clouds have been given different names depending on their appearance and the altitude at which they are found. Find out what kinds of clouds are *cirrus* clouds, *cumulus* clouds, and *stratus* clouds. What kind of clouds have the name *nimbus?*

Watch the clouds at different times of the day. What kinds of clouds form in the morning? What types of clouds that are very high in the sky do you sometimes see on a sunny day? What kinds of clouds do you see on a dark, gray day?

Fog is really a cloud that forms near the ground. Find out why it forms near the ground instead of in the sky.

Take pictures of clouds and name the different formations.

Clouds are a part of the water cycle. The drawing shows the water cycle. The clouds lose their moisture as precipitation (rain or snow). This in turn falls onto the land or water. Runoff carries water back to the oceans. Ground water seeps deep into the ground and eventually returns to the ocean. There, the water evaporates. The water vapor condenses into tiny water droplets that form clouds. On the drawing, label these steps in the water cycle: precipitation, runoff, evaporation, condensation, ground water, and ocean water.

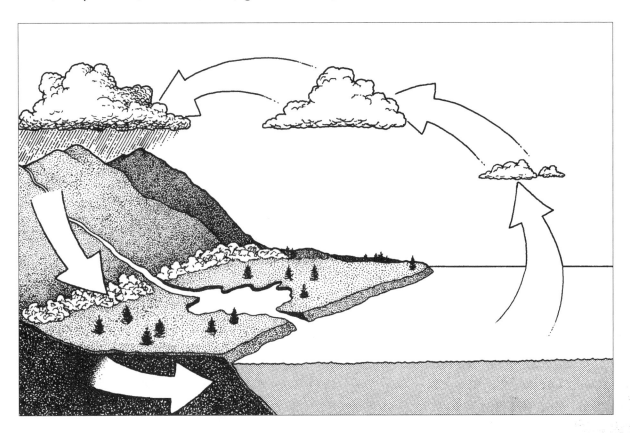

• Investigate 8—*The Greenhouse Effect* •

You may know that sunlight warms a greenhouse. This is known as the *greenhouse effect.* Not all scientists agree on what causes the greenhouse effect. Most scientists think that short-wave radiation from the sun passes through the glass of the greenhouse. As a result, these materials are warmed somewhat. The heat they give off as long-wave radiation cannot pass back through the glass of the greenhouse, and the air temperature inside the greenhouse increases. In this investigation, you will study how the greenhouse effect works.

Materials
2 plastic storage boxes
water
cardboard
heat lamp
soil
plastic wrap
2 thermometers
timer

Caution: Do not touch the bulb or bulb cover of the heat lamp. Handle the thermometers carefully.

Procedure
1. Place about 3 cm (1 inch) of soil in the bottoms of the clear plastic boxes.
2. Thoroughly moisten the soil with water.
3. Cut the cardboard to make dividers for the boxes. The cardboard should not quite reach the top of the boxes. Insert the dividers into the boxes.
4. In each box, lean the thermometer with the bulb end up against the divider.
5. Cover one box with plastic wrap.
6. Place the heat lamp about 30 cm (11.75 inches) above the boxes. Direct the light so that it shines equally on both thermometer bulbs.
7. Record the starting temperatures for both boxes in the data table on page 25.
8. Turn on the lamp and measure the temperature every minute for 15 minutes. Turn off the lamp after 15 minutes. Do not move the experiment you set up. Continue recording the temperature in both boxes for an additional 5 minutes. Leave the light off.
9. Look at the results you recorded in the data table. Answer the questions on page 25.

Light On	Temperature		Light On	Temperature		Light On	Temperature		Light Off	Temperature	
	Lid Off	Lid On		Lid Off	Lid On		Lid Off	Lid On		Lid Off	Lid On
1 min.			6 min.			11 min.			16 min.		
2 min.			7 min.			12 min.			17 min.		
3 min.			8 min.			13 min.			18 min.		
4 min.			9 min.			14 min.			19 min.		
5 min.			10 min.			15 min.			20 min.		

Observations

1. Did the temperature increase more in the covered box or the uncovered box? Why?

   _____

2. Once the light was turned off, what happened to the temperature in the

   a. covered box? _____

   b. uncovered box? _____

3. Compare the activity in the covered box to the greenhouse effect on the earth. How

   are they similar? _____

   _____

   _____

Investigate Further

Because Venus is closer to the sun than Earth, it receives almost twice the amount of solar radiation as received by Earth. Venus reflects much radiation back into space and easily absorbs heat too. Venus has surface temperatures of 460° C (864° F); Earth's highest surface temperature is about 58° C (136° F).

Earth's atmosphere is mostly nitrogen and oxygen. Venus's atmosphere is mainly carbon dioxide, with traces of water, nitrogen, and sulfuric acid. Venus's atmosphere is almost 100 times as dense as Earth's atmosphere. The solar energy easily reaches the surface of Venus. However, the thick clouds of sulfuric acid and the dense atmosphere prevent the heat from escaping, thus causing Venus's high surface temperatures.

1. How is the atmosphere of Venus like that of Earth?
2. How is the atmosphere of Venus different from that of Earth?
3. Why is the surface of Venus much hotter than the surface of Earth?

Review Unit 1

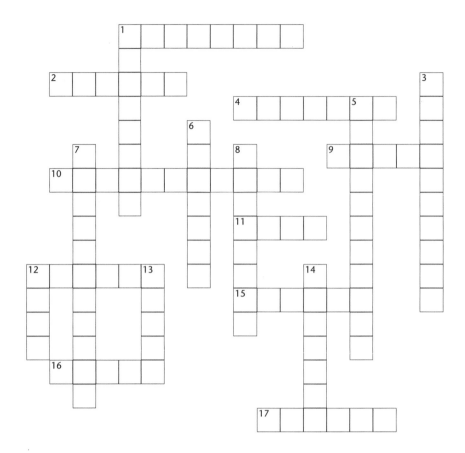

Across Clues

1. The solid substances formed naturally in the earth.
2. The layer of the earth found below the crust.
4. A supercontinent made of all the earth's continents.
9. The outermost and thinnest layer of the earth.
10. Rocks made in previously wet conditions.
11. Lacking a shiny luster.
12. They contain water and produce rain.
15. The color left by a mineral on an unglazed tile.
16. Warmer air _____.
17. The large bodies of water on the earth.

Down Clues

1. A shiny luster.
3. The large landmasses of the earth.
5. The sudden destructive movements of the earth's crust.
6. Rocks made from the hot, melted material of volcanoes.
7. Rocks made under great pressure and heat.
8. A description of how difficult a mineral is to scratch.
12. The hottest and innermost layer of the earth.
13. Cooler air _____.
14. This describes how a mineral feels.

• Investigate 1—*It's Just a Phase* •

Solids, liquids, and gases are the three forms of matter on the earth. Unlike solids and liquids, which take up a specific amount of space, a gas will spread out to fill whatever area it is given. In this investigation, you will see that how much room a gas takes up has a great deal to do with the temperature of the gas. To show this, you will make an *air thermometer.*

 Materials
small beaker, 100 ml, or other clear container
food-colored water (dark color)
soda straw (without flexible elbow)
paper clip
ice cube

Caution: Do not drink the water or reuse the straw.

 Procedure
1. Fill the container about half full with the food-colored water.
2. Put the straw in the water. Stand it straight up. You should see water move up the straw to the same height as the water in the container.
3. With the straw still in the water, bend the top end of the straw. Fold it over sharply and fasten it with the paper clip. Closing the top of the straw traps water in the bottom part of the straw and air in the top part of the straw.
4. Without squeezing the straw, lift it out of the container. If you have sealed off the top so that it is airtight, drops should form very slowly at the bottom of the straw. This is your air thermometer.
5. Watch a drop of water as it forms at the bottom of the straw. Now take an ice cube and hold it against the top part of the straw where the air is trapped. Keep watching the drop at the bottom.
6. Next, take away the ice cube. Gently place your hand around the top part of the straw. Keep watching the drop at the bottom of the straw.
7. Switch back and forth between cooling the straw with the ice cube and warming it with your hand. Note what happens to the forming drops.

Observations

1. What happened to the drop of water when the air inside the straw was cooled?

   _____

2. What must have happened to the air as it was cooled?

   _____

3. What happened to the drop of water at the bottom of the straw when you warmed the air in the straw with your hand?

   _____

   _____

4. What must have happened to the air when it was warmed?

   _____

   _____

5. What could you do to make a drop move back into the straw?

   _____

6. Why do you think this is called an air thermometer?

   _____

   _____

7. From your observations with the air thermometer, tell what happens to a gas when it is warmed.

   _____

   _____

8. What do you now know happens to a gas when it is cooled?

   _____

   _____

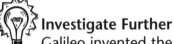

Investigate Further

Galileo invented the first air thermometer in the sixteenth century. Research information about the work of this great scientist. Watch closely some liquid-filled thermometers as the temperature changes. Explain how they work.

• Investigate 2—*Matter in Motion* •

In the previous investigation, you observed that a heated gas takes up more space than a gas that has been cooled. The molecules in any kind of matter are much too small for you to see what really happens to them when they are heated or cooled. In this investigation, however, you will *indirectly* watch how molecules move in hot and cold water.

Materials
2 small clear containers
very warm water
ice-cold water
dark-colored food coloring

Procedure
1. Pour very warm water into one of the containers until it is about three-fourths filled.
2. Pour the same amount of ice-cold water into the other container.
3. Let the two containers sit until all movement in the water has stopped.
4. When the water is still, add a drop of food coloring to each container.
5. Watch what happens in each of the containers.

Observations
1. What happened to the food coloring as soon as it was added to the cold water?

_____

_____

2. What happened to the food coloring when it was added to hot water?

_____

_____

3. Watch what happens in both containers for a minute or two. Does the food coloring mix faster in the cold water or in the hot water?

_____

_____

4. How does the cold water look after several minutes?

_____

5. How does the hot water look after several minutes?

_____

6. The food coloring is moving because the water molecules are moving. In which container must the molecules be moving faster?

_____

7. Think about how liquid-filled thermometers work. From what you observed in this investigation, explain why the liquid moves up the tube when it is warm and down the tube when it is colder?

_____

_____

Investigate Further

1. Most things take up more room when they are heated and less room when they are cooled. Why do the builders of bridges put in very long spans that will let the bridge grow or shrink?

2. Does ice take up more room or less room than water? Think of as many ways as you can to support your answer. Why is it a good thing that ice "breaks the rule"?

3. Temperature changes can make matter become larger or smaller. How have people made use of this understanding in many thermostats?

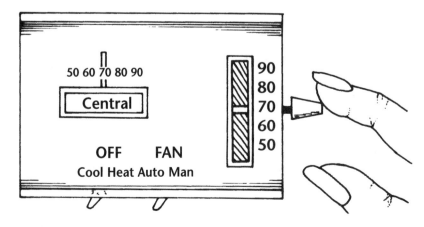

• Investigate 3—The Structure of Matter •

All matter can be divided into two main groups, *elements* and *compounds*. Elements are made up of only one kind of atom. Of the 112 elements, most can be found in nature. Examples of elements are oxygen, hydrogen, sodium, chlorine, copper, silver, and gold. The smallest part of an element that has the properties of the element is an *atom.* Each element is made up of a different kind of atom.

Compounds are substances that are made up of more than one kind of atom. Every compound contains at least two different atoms. The smallest part of a compound that has the properties of the compound is a *molecule.* One molecule of water, a common compound, for example, contains two atoms of hydrogen and one atom of oxygen. Water, salt, sugar, carbon dioxide, and rust (iron oxide) are all compounds.

In this investigation, you will use different-sized polystyrene balls as models of atoms.

Materials
2 5-cm (2-inch) polystyrene balls
1 7.5-cm (3-inch) polystyrene ball
2 toothpicks

Procedure 1
Use the small polystyrene balls as atoms of hydrogen and the large ball as an oxygen atom. Use the toothpicks to attach two atoms of hydrogen to one atom of oxygen.

Observations
1. Is your model an element or a compound? _____

2. What is the total number of atoms your model contains?_____

3. How many different elements are in your model? _____

   What are they? _____

4. How many molecules have you made?_____

5. What is the name of the substance you have made? _____

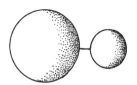

Procedure 2

Attach the large ball to one small ball with a toothpick. The large ball represents a chlorine atom; the small ball represents a sodium atom. You have just made a model of sodium chloride, which is common table salt. Many, many units of sodium chloride join together to make a single salt grain.

Observations

1. Is this new model an element or a compound? _____

2. What is the total number of atoms in your model? _____

3. How many different elements are in your model? _____

4. How many molecules have you made? _____

Summary

1. The smallest part of an element is called an _____.

2. The smallest part of a compound is a _____.

3. A substance that contains only one kind of atom is called an

   _____.

4. A substance made up of more than one kind of atom is called a

   _____.

5. _____ is formed when sodium and chlorine atoms are joined.

6. _____ is formed when two hydrogen atoms and one oxygen

   atom are joined.

7. A water molecule contains two atoms of _____.

8. A water molecule contains one atom of _____.

Investigate Further

1. Find out about the elements chlorine and sodium. Are they anything like salt as separate elements?
2. Find out about the properties of hydrogen and oxygen. Are they solids, liquids, or gases?
3. Make a study of some other elements.

• Investigate 4—*Physical Properties of Matter* •

Physical properties are characteristics of matter that can change without changing the molecules of the matter. Physical properties include such things as mass, color, shape, odor, and texture. When a type of matter changes from a solid to a liquid, this is a physical change as long as the molecules out of which it is made stay the same. In this investigation, you will look at the physical properties of several types of matter as well as some physical changes.

Materials
2 sheets of paper
2 sugar cubes
ice cube
paper towel

2 small sheets of aluminum foil
2 toothpicks
2 small containers of water

Procedure
1. Look carefully at the foil, paper, toothpicks, sugar cubes, water, and ice. Fill in the information in each box on the data table on page 35. (*State* identifies matter as a solid, liquid, or gas.)
2. Roll one of the aluminum foil sheets into a ball. Set the ball near the flat sheet of foil.
3. Tear one sheet of paper into eight strips. Put the strips on top of the other sheet of paper.
4. Break up one of the toothpicks into smaller pieces. Place the pieces near the unbroken toothpick.
5. Drop one sugar cube into one of the containers of water.
6. Let the ice cube sit on a paper towel on your desk.

Observations
1. Look at what you wrote about aluminum foil in the table. Which property of foil changed when you rolled it into a ball?

   _____

2. Did the atoms of aluminum change when you made the foil ball?_____

3. Look at the information you filled in on the paper. What property changed when you tore the paper into strips?

   _____

4. Next, look at the information you wrote about toothpicks. What property changed when you broke a toothpick into smaller pieces?

   _____

5. Look at the sugar cube you dropped into the water. What change is happening to it?

   _____

6. Look at the sugar cube still sitting on your table. Have any of its physical properties changed? If so, how?

_____

_____

7. Do you think that the molecules in the sugar cube change when they are put into water? Explain.

_____

_____

8. Do you think the water molecules are changed by adding sugar? Explain.

_____

_____

9. Can you think of a way in which you might get the sugar back again as a solid?

_____

_____

10. What is happening to the ice cube as it sits on your desk?

_____

_____

11. Which properties of the ice cube have changed?

_____

12. Do you think that the molecules in ice are the same as the ones that are in water?

_____

_____

13. All the changes you have seen are called *physical changes.* In each case, although the matter looked different from the way it began, the molecules that make it up did not change.

    On the lines below, list some other examples of physical changes.

    a. _____

    b. _____

    c. _____

Matter: Physical Properties					
Type of Matter	Color	Shape	State	Odor	Change
Aluminum Foil					
Paper					
Toothpick					
Sugar Cube					
Water					
Ice Cube					

• Investigate 5—*Chemical Properties of Matter* •

The chemical properties of matter determine how one type of matter reacts with another type of matter. One chemical property of steel wool is how it reacts with oxygen in the air. You have probably seen what happens to an iron object when it is left for a long time in moist air. The object becomes all rusty. *Rust* is a substance made of iron and oxygen atoms. In this investigation, you will watch what happens as the iron in steel wool changes to rust.

Materials

steel wool

test tube

shallow aluminum pan

pencil

small dish of vinegar

water

centimeter ruler

Caution: Handle the steel wool carefully to avoid getting splinters of steel wool in your hands.

Procedure

1. Look closely at a piece of steel wool. Fill in information about the physical properties of steel wool in the data table on page 37.
2. Roll the piece of steel wool into a ball.
3. Soak the ball of steel wool in the dish of vinegar for one minute. This removes the coating that helps keep the steel wool from rusting.
4. Squeeze out the extra vinegar from the steel wool ball.
5. Push the steel wool ball into the end of the test tube. The ball should not fall out when you turn the test tube upside down.
6. Pour water into the aluminum pie pan until it measures 1 cm ($\frac{3}{8}$ inch) in height.
7. Carefully set your test tube upside down in the water-filled pan.
8. Measure the height of the water in the bottom of the test tube. Record the measurement in the data table. Be careful not to knock your test tube over.
9. Watch the water level in the bottom of the tube. Measure the height of the water level every two minutes for twenty minutes.
10. Notice any changes that are happening to the ball of steel wool. Fill in the data table on the physical properties of the rusted steel wool.

Type of Matter	State	Color	Texture	Shape	Odor
Steel Wool					
Rusted Steel Wool					

Water Level in Centimeters										
0 Min.	2 Min.	4 Min.	6 Min.	8 Min.	10 Min.	12 Min.	14 Min.	16 Min.	18 Min.	20 Min.

Observations

1. How did the level of water in the test tube compare with the height of the water in the pan when you made your first measurement?

2. What happened to the water level in the test tube during the twenty minutes you ran your experiment?

3. What happened to the color of the ball of steel wool?

4. To form rust, iron atoms have to combine with oxygen atoms. Where does the oxygen come from that changes the iron in the steel wool to rust?

5. Explain why the water in the test tube went to a higher level as the rust formed.

6. You have just seen a chemical change. The iron in the steel wool has become rust. Which physical properties of the steel wool have changed?

Investigate Further

The world is filled with chemical changes happening all around you.
Make a list of some of the chemical changes that you see each day.

• Investigate 6—*Is It an Acid? Is It a Base?* •

Chemists have many ways of dividing matter into groups. Some kinds of substances are known as *acids,* and some are called *bases.* Other types of matter are neither acids nor bases. Acids have specific properties. Many acids, however, are not safe to taste or touch. Strong acids can eat through metal.

Bases also have special properties. They have a slippery feel and a bitter taste. Just like acids, it is not safe to touch or to taste all bases. Some are so strong that they burn the skin.

Indicators are chemicals that help tell if a substance is an acid, a base, or neither. Litmus paper is one kind of indicator. Blue litmus paper turns red in an acid. Red litmus paper turns blue in a base. In this investigation, you will use litmus paper to see if some common substances are acids or bases.

Materials
10 pieces of blue litmus paper   10 small paper cups
10 pieces of red litmus paper   marker

Ten Test Liquids
white vinegar   lemon juice
shampoo   soda water
aspirin dissolved in water   laundry detergent dissolved in water
distilled water   milk of magnesia in water
ammonia   baking soda dissolved in water

Caution: Never taste a substance used in an investigation unless directed to do so. Also make sure to wash your hands thoroughly after performing an investigation.

Procedure
1. Use the marker to write the name of each test liquid on one of the paper cups.
2. Pour a small amount of each liquid into the cup that has its name.
3. Take a piece of red litmus paper. Dip one end into the first cup.
4. Look at the wet end of the paper. Did it change color?
5. Write your results in the Red Litmus column on your table on page 39. Write *blue* if the paper turned blue. Write *same* if it did not change.
6. Next, take a piece of blue litmus paper. Dip it into the same cup. Look for a color change.
7. Did it turn *red* or stay the *same*? Write your results in the Blue Litmus column on the table.
8. Now, test each of the nine other liquids. Record your observations in the table.

SUBSTANCE	RED LITMUS	BLUE LITMUS
Vinegar		
Lemon juice		
Shampoo		
Soda water		
Aspirin water		
Laundry detergent		
Distilled water		
Milk of magnesia		
Ammonia		
Baking soda		

Observations

1. What color litmus paper changes color in acids?

_____

2. What color litmus paper changes color in bases?

_____

3. Which of the test liquids were acids?

_____

_____

4. Which of the test liquids were bases?

_____

_____

5. Which test liquid was neither an acid nor a base?

_____

• Investigate 7—The Nature of Light •

Light energy is very important to us. We are able to use our eyes because of light. Light energy also can warm our bodies. It is used to power devices such as watches and calculators. Light energy can be reflected by mirrors or shiny surfaces. When light passes from one material to another, the light we see appears to bend. The bending of light is called *refraction*. Light can pass through transparent objects. Light energy can be changed into heat energy through absorption. In this investigation, you will study some of the properties of light.

Materials

mirror	clear plastic cup	pencil	polystyrene cup
large jar lid	oatmeal box	rubber band	piece of waxed paper
pin	bubble solution		

(**Note:** 6 parts water, 1 part dish detergent, 1 teaspoon glycerin)

Procedure

1. Carefully observe your image in the mirror.

   a. Is your reflection the same size as your face? _____

   b. Are you inverted or right side up? _____

   c. Where is your right ear in your mirror image? _____

2. Fill the clear plastic cup about half full of water. Place the pencil in the water.

   Describe the appearance of the pencil. _____
   _____

3. With the pencil, punch a hole in the bottom of the polystyrene cup. Use the jar lid to get some bubble solution from your teacher. Dip the mouth of the cup into the bubble solution. Blow gently through the pencil hole.

4. Look at your reflection in the near (convex) side of the bubble.

   a. Is your image the same as in the plain mirror? _____

   b. Is your image inverted or right side up? _____

   c. Describe any other observations. _____

5. Look at your reflection in the far (concave) side of the bubble.

   a. Is your image the same as in the plain mirror? _____

   b. Is your image the same as in the convex bubble mirror? _____

   c. Is your image inverted or right side up? _____

   d. Describe any other observations. _____

6. Using the pin, poke a pinhole in the bottom of the oatmeal box. Remove the lid from the box. Pull the waxed paper tightly and place it over the open end of the box. Secure the waxed paper to the box with the rubber band. Use the pinhole camera to produce images on the waxed paper by pointing the pinhole at brightly lit objects.

For best results, the objects to be viewed should be in bright light and the camera in the dark. Try looking out of a darkened room at objects such as cars, trees, people, and buildings.

a. Describe how objects look when viewed through the camera.

_____

_____

b. How could you make the image brighter?

_____

_____

Observations

1. Light striking a mirror is bounced back, or _____.

2. Light passing through water, glass, or plastic, and air appears to make objects bend. This is called _____.

3. Concave mirrors create upside down, or _____, images.

4. Convex mirrors spread or disperse light, creating _____ images.

5. Images created by a pinhole camera are most like a _____ mirror.

Investigate Further

Make a list of some of the mirrors that you have seen. They are used in cars. Also, doctors and dentists use them. Describe the mirrors and their special uses. What is the largest mirror that you know about? What is the strangest mirror that you have seen?

• Investigate 8—*Getting Charged Up* •

Part 1

Most of us are familiar with static electricity. Static electricity causes the clothes from the dryer to cling together. Have you ever gotten a shock when you touched metal after you walked across a carpet? That was caused by static electricity. Your walking made electrons in the carpet and your body more active. When your charged body touched the metal, the extra electrons jumped from your finger. The movement of electrons from one place to another is an *electric current*. Currents from static electricity are not easy to control. An electrical current from a battery is predictable and easy to use. In this investigation, you will see that some materials conduct low-voltage electricity, while others do not. A material that does not conduct low-voltage electricity may conduct high-voltage electricity.

Materials

copper penny	aluminum foil	chalk
rubber (comb)	glass	unpainted wood
plastic fork	pencil lead	
paper clip	wood pencil	cardboard
lamp socket	bulb for socket	2 1.5-volt D batteries
3 pieces of wire (20 cm)		2 nails

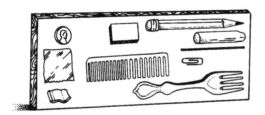
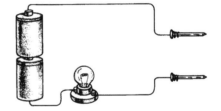

Caution: Always be very cautious when working with electricity. Do so only with adult supervision.

Procedure

1. Glue or paste samples of the first ten items listed on a piece of cardboard.
2. Make a conductivity indicator from the batteries, wire, nails, bulb, and socket.
3. Test to see that the bulb works by touching the two nails together. If the indicator lights up, then it is working properly.
4. Test each of the items by placing the nails on each sample. Be careful not to touch the nails together. If the bulb lights up, then the material will conduct low-voltage electricity.
5. List each item in the data table on page 43. Place a check mark in the appropriate column to indicate whether the material is a conductor or not.

Material Tested	Conductor	Nonconductor

Observations

1. Divide the materials into two groups: conductors and nonconductors. List the members of each group in the following chart.

Conductors	Nonconductors

2. What is one property that most of the conductors seem to have?

_____

Investigate Further

List as many uses of conductors in your home as you can find. Research the new field of "superconductors." Make a list of their possible uses.

Part 2

Sources of electricity (batteries), conductors (wires), and electrical devices (light bulbs) can be connected in various combinations. Not all connections will result in a closed circuit (the bulb lights). When a circuit sends the electricity directly back to the electrical source, a "short" circuit occurs. Short circuits can be dangerous because of the buildup of heat. In this investigation, you will study electrical circuits.

Materials
2 1.5-volt D batteries
2 flashlight bulbs
1.5 meters (5 feet) of common bell wire, cut into needed lengths

Caution: Always be very cautious when working with electricity. Do so only with adult supervision.

Procedure
1. Look at each circuit diagram.
2. Predict whether or not you think the bulb or bulbs will light.
3. Construct each circuit.
4. Write a description of what happens.

a. Will the bulb light? _____

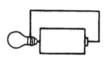

Results: _____

b. Will the bulb light? _____

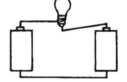

Results: _____

c. Will the bulbs light? _____

Results: _____

d. Will the bulb light? _____

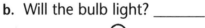

Results: _____

e. Will the bulb light? _____

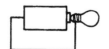

Results: _____

f. Will the bulb light? _____

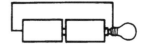

Results: _____

g. Will the bulb light? _____

Results: _____

h. Will the bulbs light? _____

Results: _____

i. Will the bulb light? _____

Results: _____

j. Will the bulb light? _____

Results: _____

k. Will the bulb light? _____

Results: _____

l. Will the bulb light? _____

Results: _____

Observations

1. Will all combinations make the bulb or bulbs light? _____

2. What common connections are characteristic of a closed circuit?

_____

_____

_____

3. Did any of the connections become hot? If so, which ones? This indicates a short circuit.

_____

_____

Investigate Further

Do some research to determine how our homes and schools are protected from short circuits. Construct a model circuit demonstrating the use of fuses.

UNIT 2

Part 1

A type of stone that can be found on earth has the unusual ability to attract pieces of iron. It is called *lodestone,* or *magnetite.* It is an "iron oxide." Lodestone is a natural magnet. Magnets do not attract all materials. Magnets attract some substances more than others. In this investigation, you will study how magnetism works.

Materials

magnet	sheet of plastic	copper sheet	piece of cloth
aluminum foil	sheet of paper	piece of wood	waxed paper
paper clip	glass pane	steel sheet	emery cloth

Procedure

1. Place each object, one at a time, next to the magnet. Record whether or not the object is magnetic by writing *yes* or *no* in the following data table.
2. Place each object, one at a time, between the magnet and the paper clip. Record in the data table whether or not magnetism will pass through the object.

Object	Magnetic?	Does Magnetism Pass Through?
Sheet of plastic		
Copper sheet		
Piece of cloth		
Aluminum foil		
Sheet of paper		
Piece of wood		
Waxed paper		
Paper clip		
Glass pane		
Steel sheet		
Emery cloth		

Observations

1. What conclusions can you make about objects that are attracted to magnets?

_____

_____

2. What conclusions can you make about magnetism passing through objects?

_____

Investigate Further

Collect a variety of different magnets, such as horseshoe, bar, and round magnets. Place each magnet on a flat surface; cover it with a sheet of paper. Sprinkle iron filings on the paper. Observe the magnetic lines of force. Sketch these patterns.

Part 2

Although magnetism and electricity are not the same type of energy, they are related. Where there is electricity flowing, you will usually find a magnetic field. A changing electric current produces a magnetic field. Electricity, in fact, can be used to make a type of magnet called an *electromagnet*. An electromagnet acts just as if it were a normal magnet, except that it is only magnetic as long as there is an electric current flowing. In this investigation, you will make an electromagnet.

Materials

1.5 meters (5 feet) of bell wire	10-cm (4-inch) long nail	6-volt battery
1.5-volt D battery	20 paper clips	

Procedure

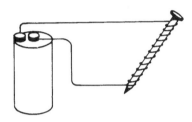

1. Remove about 3 cm (about 1 inch) of insulation from each end of the wire.
2. Wrap the wire around the nail. Leave 20 cm (8 inches) of unwrapped wire at each end.
3. Connect the ends of the wire to the positive and negative terminals of the 1.5-volt battery. It does not matter which end is connected to which terminal.
4. Test your electromagnet. Hold the head of the nail near a pile of paper clips and observe what happens.
5. Count the number of paper clips that the electromagnet picks up.
6. Connect the electromagnet to the 6-volt battery. Repeat Steps 4 and 5.
7. Remove the wire from the electromagnet and cut the wire in half. Rewind the electromagnet and again connect it to the 1.5-volt battery. Repeat Steps 4 and 5.
8. Connect the electromagnet to the 6-volt battery. Repeat Steps 4 and 5.

Observations

1. How many paper clips did the electromagnet pick up when connected to

    a. the 1.5-volt battery with the longer wire? _____

    b. the 6-volt battery with the longer wire? _____

    c. the 1.5-volt battery with the shorter wire? _____

    d. the 6-volt battery with the shorter wire? _____

2. The _____ battery allows the electromagnet to pick up a greater number of paper clips.

3. The more turns of wire on an electromagnet, the _____ paper clips it will pick up.

Review Unit 2

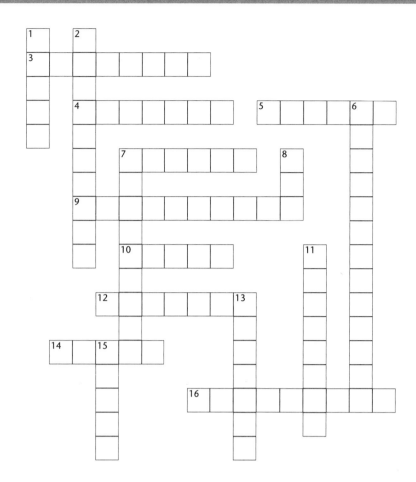

Across Clues

3. The type of change that makes the substance a new kind of matter.

4. To bounce back light.

5. A mirror that curves toward you.

7. Form of matter that takes the shape of its container.

9. They help tell if a substance is an acid or a base.

10. A circuit that can produce a dangerous buildup of heat.

12. A mirror that curves away from you.

14. They feel slippery and have a bitter taste.

16. Cooler air shrinks, or _____.

Down Clues

1. They have a sour taste and strong ones can dissolve metal.

2. The bending of light.

6. A temporary magnet powered by electricity.

7. A natural magnet.

8. It spreads out to fill its container.

11. Observable properties of matter that can change without changing the molecules of the matter.

13. Warmer air spreads out, or _____.

15. Form of matter with its own shape.

Mid-Book Test

A Use the terms in the box to complete the sentences.

mantle	crust	core
lithosphere	plates	Richter scale
minerals	sedimentary rock	metamorphic rock
igneous rock	precipitation	evaporation
condensation	greenhouse effect	

1. The outer layer of the earth is called the _____.

2. The process by which liquid water turns to vapor is called _____.

3. Rock formed from the hardening of hot, melted rock of volcanoes is called

   _____.

4. The layer of the earth between the crust and the core is called the

   _____.

5. _____ are naturally occurring, solid substances in the earth.

6. The trapping of heat by the atmosphere near the surface of the earth is known as the

   _____.

7. The topmost solid part of the earth is called the _____.

8. Rock formed when water glues soil and sand together is called _____.

9. The lithosphere is broken into a number of large pieces called _____.

10. The changing of water vapor back into a liquid is called _____.

11. Rock formed by great heat and pressure is called _____.

12. An instrument used to measure the strength of an earthquake is the

    _____.

13. The innermost layer of the earth is called the _____.

14. Another name for rain and snow is _____.

TEST

B Write the letter of the best answer in the blank.

_____ 1. A phase of matter that completely fills its container is a
- **a.** solid.
- **b.** liquid.
- **c.** compound.
- **d.** gas.

_____ 2. The smallest part of an element is
- **a.** an atom.
- **b.** a molecule.
- **c.** a compound.
- **d.** a liquid.

_____ 3. Salt dissolving in water is an example of
- **a.** a chemical change.
- **b.** a physical change.
- **c.** an element.
- **d.** a litmus test.

_____ 4. Red litmus paper is turned blue by
- **a.** an element.
- **b.** an acid.
- **c.** a base.
- **d.** water.

_____ 5. A changing electric current produces
- **a.** a short circuit.
- **b.** refraction.
- **c.** a lodestone.
- **d.** a magnetic field.

C Indicate whether the bulb or bulbs will light up by writing *yes* or *no* above each picture.

1. _____

2. _____

3. _____

4. _____

5. _____

6. _____

• Investigate 1—*It's Alive!* •

Living things possess certain characteristics that nonliving things do not have. In this investigation, you will look at some objects that are living and at some that are not. After comparing the objects, you may be able to determine what it means to be alive.

Materials

piece of wood	yeast in water
seashell	bone
fish in water	worm
stone	bread mold
paper clip	cotton ball
insect	wild strawberry with runners
	(or other plant with runners)

Procedure

1. Carefully examine each object.
2. Decide whether each object is living or nonliving. Record your decisions in the data table on page 52.
3. If you have decided that an object is alive, think about the characteristics of that living thing that helped you make your decision. Record these characteristics in the data table.

Specimen	Living or Nonliving	Characteristics of Living Things
Wood		
Yeast		
Shell		
Bone		
Fish		
Worm		
Stone		
Mold		
Paper clip		
Cotton ball		
Insect		
Plant		

Observations

1. What are some characteristics found in living things but not in nonliving things?

_____

_____

2. Based on this investigation, write a sentence that describes what it means to be alive.

_____

_____

Investigate Further

Look around your home. Make a list of living and nonliving items. Compare your list with the lists made by your classmates.

• Investigate 2—*Investigating Competition* •

We all understand competition in sports or games. Each person wants to win. Competition may not be so easily understood when you look at plants growing in a field. All plants need sunlight, water, minerals, and space. They compete for these things. Some plants survive and produce seeds, which are the next generation. Some die, or they are small and produce only a few seeds. In this investigation, you will find out how plants compete for what they need.

Materials
4 small plastic flowerpots or paper cups   metric ruler
marker   potting soil
15 tomato seeds   15 radish seeds
water   plastic wrap

Procedure
1. Measure 3 cm (about 1 inch) from the top of each pot or cup. Make a mark. Note: If cups are used, punch three holes in the bottom of each cup for drainage.
2. Fill each pot up to the mark with soil.
3. Dampen the soil.
4. Place the seeds on the soil and push down gently.
   Pot 1—1 tomato, 1 radish
   Pot 2—2 tomatoes, 2 radishes
   Pot 3—4 tomatoes, 4 radishes
   Pot 4—8 tomatoes, 8 radishes
5. Cover the seeds with a small amount of soil. Dampen the soil with water.
6. Cover the pots with plastic wrap. Place them in a sunny spot.
7. After seven or eight days, remove the plastic wrap. Gently lift the seedlings from the soil.
8. Select two typical plants from each pot. Measure each plant from root to tip. Also measure the length of one leaf on each of the two plants.
9. Record your observations in the data table on page 54.

Pot		Length of Plant	Length of Leaf	Number of Plants That Grew	Color
1	Tomato				
	Radish				
2	Tomato				
	Radish				
3	Tomato				
	Radish				
4	Tomato				
	Radish				

Observations

1. In which pot are the radish plants largest?

   _____

2. In which pot are the tomato plants largest?

   _____

3. In which pot are the radish plants smallest?

   _____

4. In which pot are the tomato plants smallest?

   _____

5. In which pot did the most competition take place?

   _____

6. Was one kind of plant more successful than the other? Explain your answer.

   _____

   _____

7. Why do you think people weed their gardens?

   _____

   _____

• Investigate 3—*Can I Make a Difference?* •

People change natural environments in many ways. Some examples include plowing up meadows, cutting down forests, clearing land for development, running factories and cars that pollute the air, and filling landfills with garbage. Most of these activities add materials to the air and water that can be harmful to living things. Such materials are called *pollutants*. Air and water that contain pollutants are said to be polluted. Polluted air and water can cause sickness and death for the earth's living things, including people. In this investigation, you will find out if there are pollutants in the waters where you live. You will learn where these pollutants come from and what you can do about pollution.

Materials

jar of tap water	jar of pond water
jar of puddle water or melted snow	jar of stream water
filter paper	funnel
magnifying glass	shallow pan
pH test paper	4 petri dishes
Elodea	4 large test tubes

Caution: Collect water samples only when accompanied by an adult. Never drink the water you collect, and always wash your hands after completing an investigation.

folded filter paper

Procedure

Complete the following six tests for each water sample. Fill in the data table on page 56 as you obtain your results.

> **Test 1:** Hold the jar of water up to the light. What color is it?
>
> **Test 2:** Smell the water.
>
> **Test 3:** Pour some of the sample through a filter paper that has been folded to fit inside a funnel. (Fold the filter paper in half; fold in half again; open it; and place it in a funnel.) Allow the water to drain into a pan. Use a magnifying glass. Look at what remains on the filter paper.

Test 4: Use pH paper to test if the water is too acidic for organisms. Your teacher will help you with this procedure.

Test 5: Place a small amount of each sample in a petri dish. Use the magnifying glass to look for tiny animals or plants.

Test 6: Place a sprig of *Elodea* in a test tube filled with each sample. Place all of the test tubes in a sunny spot for three days.

Test	Tap Water	Pond Water	Puddle Water or Snow	Stream Water
1				
2				
3				
4				
5				
6				

Observations

1. If the sample is cloudy, is it polluted? _____

   What do you think the pollutant is? _____

2. If the sample smells bad, is it polluted? _____

   What do you think the pollutant is? _____

   _____

3. Where did any articles trapped by the filter come from? _____

   _____

4. Is the water too acidic for many pond and stream organisms to survive in?

_____

5. The presence of many tiny algae in ponds or streams shows that the water is polluted with fertilizers from surrounding fields and lawns. Is your pond or stream water polluted with fertilizer?

_____

6. In which sample does _Elodea_ grow best? Why?

_____

7. Do you think that water in which _Elodea_ grows best is healthy for humans? Why?

_____

8. Is the tap water polluted? Why or why not?

_____

9. If the water in your local pond or stream is polluted, what can you do to clean it up? Think about what pollutants are in the water and how they got there.

_____

_____

Investigate Further
Look at your answer to question 9 above. Choose one activity and perform it with the help of an adult for a week. After the week is over, discuss how you and your classmates have helped improve the water quality in your pond or stream. Would you be willing to continue to fight pollution? What might happen if everyone made an effort?

Things are grouped together, or classified, according to characteristics they have in common. For example, you will usually find all the milk in a supermarket in the same location, large bottles of 2-percent milk may be on one shelf, and small ones on another. Skim milk may be put on shelves next to the 2-percent milk.

Living things are also classified. It makes them much easier to study. Classification also shows how closely organisms are related to each other. The largest classification group of living things is called a *kingdom.* Organisms in kingdoms may be divided into *phyla.* Phyla are divided into *classes*; classes into *orders*; orders into *families*; families into *genera.* Finally, genera may be divided into *species.* Members of the same specifies are very similar; for example, dogs. The more similar organisms are, the more classification levels they share. All dogs share every classification level from kingdom to species. In this investigation, you will group some fasteners into kingdoms, phyla, classes, and orders.

Materials
nail—#1	safety pin—#2	latch—#3
straight pin—#4	lock—#5	screw—#6
paste—#7	glue—#8	hook & eye—#9
button—#10	snap—#11	zipper—#12
tape—#13	paper for labels	

Procedure
1. Place objects #1, 2, 3, 4, 5, 6, 9, 11, and 12 together. What characteristics do the objects share?

   _____

2. Label these objects "Kingdom I."

3. Place the rest of the objects together. How do they differ from objects in Kingdom I?

   _____

4. Label these objects "Kingdom II."

5. Divide the objects from Kingdom I into two phyla and label.

   Phylum A–#2, 4, 9, 11, 12. What characteristic do they share?

   _____

   Phylum B–#1, 3, 5, 6. How do they differ from the objects in Phylum A?

   _____

6. Divide the objects from Phylum A into two classes and label.

Class 1–#2, 4. What characteristics do they share?_____

Class 2–#9, 11, 12. How do they differ from the objects in Class 1?

_____

7. Divide the objects from Class 1 into two orders and label.

Order a–#2. Order b–#4. How do they differ?_____

_____

8. Now divide the objects from Kingdom II into two phyla and label.

Phylum C–#7, 8, 13. What characteristics do they share?_____

Phylum D–#10. How does this object differ from those in Phylum C? _____

_____

9. Divide the objects from Phylum C into two classes and label.

Class 1–#7, 8. What characteristics do they share?_____

Class 2–#13. How does this object differ from those in Class 1? _____

_____

10. Divide the objects from Phylum C Class 1 into two orders and label. How do

they differ? _____

_____

Observations

1. What object is found in Phylum D? _____

2. If objects are in the same class, they are also in the same_____

and _____.

3. If two or more objects were in an order, they could be divided into

_____.

4. The classification level in this investigation that had the most closely related objects

was the _____.

5. In nature, the classification level having the most closely related organisms is the

_____.

• Investigate 5—*A Look at a Plant Cell* •

Plants and animals are alike in many ways. Both groups are living things. They both reproduce and grow, need sources of energy, and give off waste products. However, animals and plants are different. Plants are able to produce their own food from light. Most animals are more complex than plants. Plant cells and animal cells are also similar and yet different. Each cell has a "brain" called the *nucleus*. All cells have a thin "skin," or *cell membrane*. Plant cells, however, also have a thick, nonliving *cell wall*. Animal cells do not have a cell wall. In this investigation, you will study plant cells.

Materials
onion	tweezers
microscope slide	water
medicine dropper	cover slip
microscope	

Procedure
1. Separate the onion piece into its layers.
2. Use the tweezers to peel off a very thin piece of onion skin from the inside of a layer.
3. Put a piece of the thin onion skin on a slide.
4. Use a medicine dropper to add a drop of water.
5. Put the cover slip on.
6. Observe the onion skin with the microscope.

Observations
1. Draw the cells that you see. Label the cell wall.
2. Describe the shape of the cells.

_____

_____

Investigate Further
If your teacher has some prepared slides, look at some different types of tissues or cells. Try to identify each slide sample as cells from either a plant or an animal. Remember, plant cells have a cell wall, but animal cells do not. Check your answers with your teacher.

• Investigate 6—A Look at an Animal Cell •

All living things contain cells. Cells are microscopic and are made of living materials. Cells have many different sizes, shapes, and purposes. Skin cells act as a covering. Nerve cells send and receive messages. Blood cells move materials from place to place. In this investigation, you will study human skin cells.

Materials
medicine dropper
microscope slide
methylene blue
microscope

water
flat toothpick
cover slip

Caution: Never share toothpicks. Throw away the toothpicks after you place the cheek material on the slide. Handle only your own slide. Thoroughly wash your hands after this and all investigations.

Procedure
1. Use a medicine dropper to place a drop of water on a clean slide.
2. Gently scrape the inside of your cheek with the blunt end of the toothpick.
3. Mix the cheek material from the end of the toothpick in the drop of water on the slide.
4. Add a drop of methylene blue.
5. Cover the slide with a cover slip.
6. Observe the cells with the microscope.

Observations
1. Draw the cells that you see.

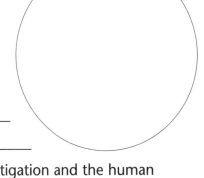

2. Describe the human cheek cells as seen with

   the microscope. _____

   _____

3. How are the onion cells that you viewed in the last investigation and the human

   cells different? _____

4. How are the onion cells that you viewed in the last investigation and the human

   cells alike? _____

Investigate Further
You have examined human cheek cells. Find out how these cells look in comparison to other human cells. How are all human cells alike? How are different types of human cells different? For example, do muscles cells look like cheek skin cells?

Part 1

The following items describe animals. Read each riddle. Put your answer in the puzzle at the bottom of the page.

1. We are social insects. Like other social insects, we live together in colonies. We build hills and are often accused of ruining people's picnics. We can lift weights that are heavier than we are. There is an animal with a long, sticky tongue that likes to eat us.

2. I am a marsupial. Marsupial mothers give birth to undeveloped babies. As a result, I have a pouch in which I carry my young until they are more developed. My babies are called *joeys*. All of us hop on our long back legs and use our long tails for balance when hopping. I live in Australia.

3. I am a large cat. I live in a group with males, females, and cubs. Our group is called a *pride*. I have been called the "king of the jungle."

4. I am a small bird. I can fly quickly backwards, forward, and up or down. I have a long, thin beak, which helps me drink nectar from flowers.

5. I am a reptile. I move along by sliding on my belly because I do not have legs. I can "smell" with my tongue, which is forked. Like other reptiles, I am cold-blooded, which means my body temperature changes with the temperature of my environment.

6. I am a large mammal that looks like a fish and lives in the ocean. Unlike fish, I breathe air through lungs. I must come to the surface of the water to breathe air. Like other mammals, I have some hair, give birth to live babies, and am warm-blooded. Because I am warm-blooded, my body temperature stays about the same even though the temperature of my surroundings changes.

7. I am a cartilaginous fish that lives in the ocean. Many other kinds of fish, such as trout, have bony skeletons, but my skeleton is made of cartilage. I am a meat-eating fish and have several rows of teeth. Many people fear me.

1.   A __ __ __

2.   __ __ N __ __ __ __ __

3.   __ I __ __

4.   __ __ __ M __ __ __ __ __ __ __

5.   __ __ A __ __

6.   __ __ __ L __

7.   S __ __ __ __

Part 2

Animals cannot make their own food. They do not produce their own energy sources. Animals are known as consumers. They consume a variety of foods. Some animals eat grass. Other animals eat nuts and berries. Animals that eat plants are called *herbivores.* Many animals eat meat by eating other animals. Meat-eating animals are called *carnivores.* Bears are one type of animal, called an *omnivore,* that eats both plants and animals. They like to eat fish, including salmon.

This is a monthly record of the number of salmon eaten by one bear in a year.

January	2
February	1
March	10
April	12
May	20
June	25
July	30
August	35
September	30
October	20
November	10
December	5

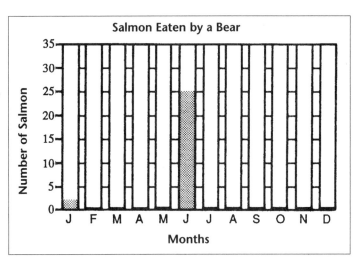

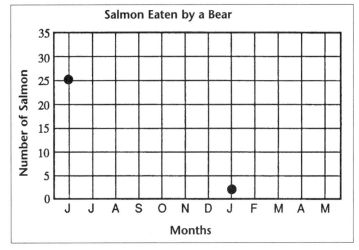

Procedure

1. Record the data above on the bar graph and the line graph. January's and June's data have already been shown on each graph as an example. Notice that the bar graph begins with January and the line graph begins with June.
2. Complete the line graph by connecting the dots after you record the data.

Observations

1. In which month did the bear eat the most salmon? _____

2. During which season did the bear eat the fewest salmon?

   _____ summer   _____ fall   _____ winter   _____ spring

3. Bears sleep, or hibernate, through much of one season. Based on the graphed information, what season do you think they sleep through? Explain your answer.

   _____

• Investigate 8—*A Look at the Plant Kingdom* •

Part 1

Seeds can be found in all shapes, sizes, and colors. Fruits contain seeds. The next time you eat an orange, apple, pear, or banana, look very closely at the seeds. A seed can grow into plants. The seed has an *embryo*, or baby plant, inside. Seeds also contain *cotyledons*, or seed leaves. These seed leaves provide food for the embryo. In this investigation, you will study how seeds grow.

Materials

jar	blotter paper
newspaper	bean seeds
corn seeds	water

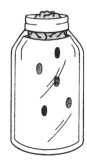

Procedure

1. Curl the blotter paper around the inside of the jar.
2. Crumple a piece of newspaper. Wedge the newspaper into the top of the jar so that the blotter paper is pushed against the sides of the jar.
3. Place a few bean and corn seeds between the sides of the jar and the blotter paper.
4. Add water until it touches the bottom 2 cm ($\frac{3}{4}$ inch) of the blotter paper. The blotter paper should soak up the water.
5. Do not cover the seeds with water. Add water as needed to keep the blotter paper moist.
6. Look at the seeds every day.

Observations

1. Which part of the plants grew first? _____
2. Did that part grow up or down? _____
3. Which part of the plants grew next? _____
4. Did that part grow up or down? _____
5. What happened to the cotyledons, or seed leaves, as the plants grew?

   _____

6. When the cotyledons die, how do the new plants get food?

   _____

Investigate Further

Plant the sprouting seeds and watch them grow. Record your observations in a journal.

Part 2

Many plants produce seeds. New plants can grow from the seeds. Seeds sometimes are exposed to harsh conditions. A seed might be baked by the sun or frozen by the cold. Water and wind can carry the seed far from its parent plant. Animals can swallow a seed and later expel it as waste. In this investigation, you will compare the growth of different seeds.

Materials
100 bean or corn seeds per group   water
container for soaking   paper plates
paper towels

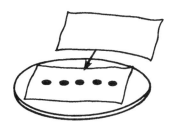

Procedure
1. Soak the seeds overnight.
2. Divide the seeds among the members of your group. For example, 10 students would have 10 seeds each; or 5 students would have 20 seeds each.
3. Place a moistened paper towel on the paper plate.
4. Arrange your seeds so that there is room between them.
5. Cover the seeds with another paper towel.
6. Add water to your "garden" as necessary.
7. Count the number of sprouted seeds every day.
8. Complete the data table and bar graph. Use your group's data over a ten-day period.

	Experiment Days									
	1	2	3	4	5	6	7	8	9	10
Number of Sprouts on Your Plate	0									
Number of Sprouts for Entire Group	0									

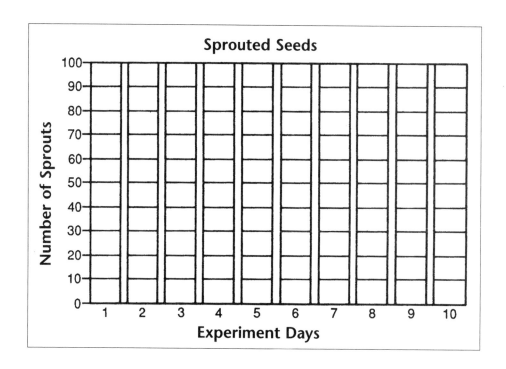

Sprouted Seeds

Number of Sprouts

Experiment Days

Observations

1. Did all of the seeds sprout? _____

2. On what day did the first seed sprout? _____

3. How many sprouts did you get from 100 seeds or beans? _____

4. Why do plants produce so many seeds? _____

_____

Investigate Further

There are many different kinds of seeds. You could repeat this experiment with different varieties of seeds. Seeds for eating are not chemically treated for fungus protection. Try sprouting treated and untreated seeds. Is there any difference in the number of seeds that sprout?

• Investigate 9—*A Look at Microorganisms* •

Part 1

Some microorganisms are plantlike and some are animal-like. Some bacteria and algae are like plants in that they can make their own food. Amoebas, paramecia, and *Euglena* are like animals since they can move around and capture food. *Euglena* also can make their own food like plants. In this investigation, you will look at microscopic organisms.

Materials

microscope depression slide
medicine dropper
magnifying lens

jar of pond water
cover slip
microscope

Caution: Never collect pond water without adult supervision. Avoid touching the pond water. Wash your tools and hands thoroughly after completing the investigation.

Procedure

1. Use a medicine dropper to place a drop of pond water on your microscope slide.
2. Cover the water droplet with a cover slip.
3. Observe the water drop with the magnifying lens.
4. Look at the drop of pond water with the microscope.
5. Move the slide until you see some microscopic organisms.
6. Sketch and describe the microorganisms you see.

Observations

Describe the organisms and comment on what they were doing.

_____

_____

Investigate Further

Microscopic organisms can be helpful or harmful. Investigate this topic and make a list of microorganisms that either benefit or harm people.

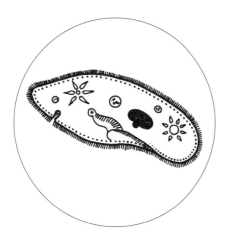

Paramecium

Amoeba

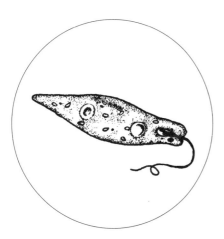

Euglena

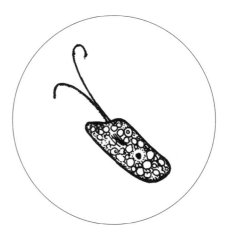

Chilomonas

Vorticella

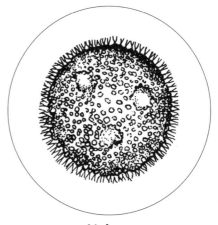

Volvox

Part 2

Some algae are so small that you can see them only when millions of them are in the same place. Most algae have some green. This is because they can produce their own food. Algae can be found in fresh water and salt water. Diatoms are a type of algae. The cell walls of diatoms are made of silica. When a diatom dies, its silica shell is all that is left. In this investigation, you will look at diatom shells that are part of silver polish.

Materials

medicine dropper   water
microscope slide   toothpick
silver polish   microscope

Procedure

1. Use an medicine dropper to place a drop of water on your microscope slide.
2. Dip your toothpick into the jar of silver polish.
3. Swirl the silver polish into the drop of water.
4. Use the low power of your microscope. Look at the polish.
5. Draw some of the diatoms that you see.

Observations

1. Are all of the diatoms shaped alike? _____

2. Compare your sketches with those of your classmates. Were the diatoms they drew shaped like yours? What conclusions can you make about the shape of diatoms?

_____

_____

_____

Investigate Further

Algae live in many environments. With the help of an adult, collect some water and soil from streams, ponds, and large bodies of water. Make slides to observe with the microscope. See whether you can detect any live forms of microscopic plants.

• Investigate 10—*Bubble, Bubble, Toil, and Trouble* •

Fungi are organisms such as yeasts, molds, and mushrooms. They are rooted to one spot like plants, but they cannot make their own food. Fungi get their food from rotting plant and animal matter. Fungi are known as *decomposers*. Mushrooms are well-known fungi. Some mushrooms can be eaten. Molds are also fungi. The medicine penicillin is produced by bread mold. Yeast is another kind of fungi. Yeast is used to bake bread. In this investigation, you will study the heat given off by yeast.

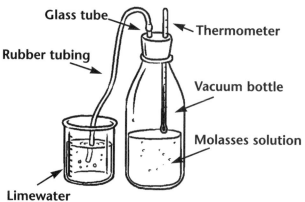

Materials

2 thermometers	2 rubber tubings (35 cm)
2 vacuum bottles	2 hole stoppers (to fit the bottles)
dry yeast	2 glass tubes (8 cm)
2 250-ml beakers	400 ml of molasses (25% solution in water)
300 ml of limewater	

Procedure

1. Assemble two setups like the one shown in the diagram.
2. Lubricate the thermometers. Insert each one into one of the holes in each stopper. Place a glass tube in the second hole in each stopper.
3. Pour 200 ml of molasses solution into each bottle.
4. Pour 150 ml of limewater into each beaker. Place the other end of the rubber tubing for each setup into one of the beakers.
5. Add $\frac{1}{4}$ package of dry yeast to just one of the bottles.
6. Mix the yeast with the molasses solution by swirling the bottle.
7. Begin reading the thermometer in each setup. Record the temperature data over a 48-hour period. Take readings from the thermometers as frequently as possible.
8. Graph the results of this experiment. Plot the results of both setups on the same graph on page 71.

Thermometer Data

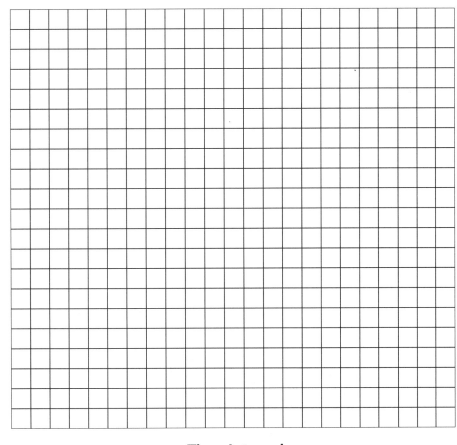

Temperature °F

Time Interval

Observations

1. In which bottle did the temperature become higher? _____

2. Explain the graphed data for the bottle with yeast. _____

   _____

3. Explain the graphed data for the bottle without yeast. _____

   _____

Investigate Further

Yeast is used in the fermentation processes. Research information about the process in a reference book or on the World Wide Web. Write a report about the various uses of the fermentation process. Before you begin writing, organize your information and prepare an outline for the report. Also, you could set up various experiments using different concentrations of molasses and yeast.

• Investigate 11—*Building Blocks of Living Things* •

Just as bricks are the building blocks of buildings, cells are the building blocks of organisms. Most plants and animals are made from millions of cells. However, some microscopic organisms—like amoebas, yeast, and bacteria—are unicellular, or have only one cell. Unlike bricks, cells do much more than just build the structure. All of the things that microorganisms do are also carried out in the cell.

The nucleus is the control center of the cell. All of the information about what the cell should do or how it should act is stored there. The cell membrane allows materials to move in and out of the cell. A vacuole is a bubble that may contain food or water. There are many other structures in the cell, but a powerful electron microscope must be used to see them. In this investigation, you will compare plant, animal, and amoeba cells.

 Materials
cell drawings

Low Power   High Power
Elodea Plant

Low Power   High Power
Onion

 Procedure
Compare the cell drawings.

Amoeba

Human Cheek Cells

 Observations

1. Describe the plant cells.

_____

2. Describe the animal cells.

_____

3. Describe the amoeba.

_____

4. What are the main differences between the plant cells and the cheek cells?

_____

5. What are the main differences between the cheek cells and the amoeba?

_____

_____

6. What are the main differences between the plant cells and the amoeba?

_____

_____

7. What do all plant cells have in common?

_____

8. Plant cells have green structures called *chloroplasts*. They are the sugar-producing factories of the cell. Why do you think animals and amoebas cannot make their own food?

_____

_____

9. Why do almost all cells have nuclei and cell membranes?

_____

_____

Investigate Further
If a compound microscope is available, make wet-mount slides of a wood shaving and of a thin layer of cells peeled from an onion. Look at a prepared slide of frog blood cells, if available. Draw and label what you see.

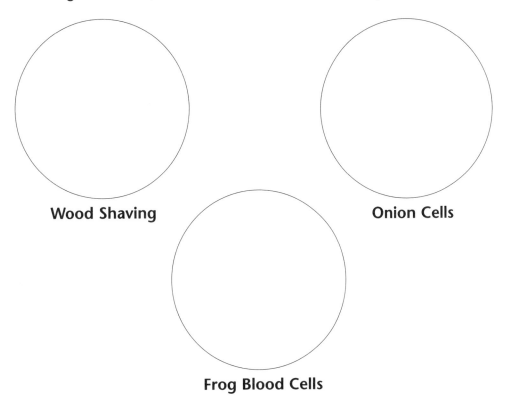

Wood Shaving

Onion Cells

Frog Blood Cells

Review Unit 3

Across Clues

2. An organism, such as a fungus, that gets its food from rotting or decomposing material.
4. The thick outermost layer of a plant cell is known as the cell _____.
7. Algae from which silver polish is made.
9. Also known as seed leaves.
11. Organisms, such as animals, that must eat to get food.
13. An organism able to produce its own food.
14. The "brain," or control center, of a cell.
15. To group things according to their characteristics.

Down Clues

1. Yeast and mold are examples of these.
3. The building blocks of living things.
5. The part of a seed that is the "baby" plant.
6. The largest grouping of the classification system.
8. A tool used to see extremely small organisms.
10. Harmful materials in our surroundings.
12. The thin "skin" of a cell.

• Investigate 1—*Why Plants Don't Get Hungry* •

All living things need food for energy to stay alive. Animals get energy by eating plants and other animals. Plants make their own food. Their food-making process is called *photosynthesis*. Energy from the sun allows green plants to turn water (absorbed through the roots) and carbon dioxide (a gas in the air) into sugar. Sugar is the plant's food. As this process is going on, oxygen is given off as a waste product. In this investigation, you will find out what happens to a plant if it cannot make its own food and how that can happen.

Materials

iodine	geranium (or other potted plant)
paper clips	boiled water
2 beakers	tweezers
rubbing alcohol	hot plate
oven mitts	petri dish
11-cm (4-inch) squares of black paper	

Caution: Use the hot plate only with adult supervision. Never heat alcohol over a flame. Use oven mitts when handling the hot plate and beakers.

Procedure

1. Fold the black paper squares over two or more of the leaves on the plant. Hold the squares in place with paper clips.
2. Put the plant in the sun for three days.
3. After three days, pinch the covered leaves from the plant. Remove the black paper.
4. Put the leaves into a beaker of boiled water and allow the leaves to become limp.
5. Use the tweezers to remove the leaves from the water. Put them into a beaker that is half full of alcohol. Heat the leaves and alcohol on a hot plate until the green color disappears from the leaves.
   Important: Do not heat the alcohol over a flame.

6. Place the leaves in a petri dish. Cover them with iodine. If food is present, the leaf will turn black.

7. Repeat Steps 3–6. This time use the same number of leaves that were not covered.

Observations

1. What color are the paper-covered leaves? _____

2. What color are the uncovered leaves? _____

3. What do the uncovered leaves contain? _____

4. What did the black paper keep away from the covered leaves?

_____

5. Write two or three sentences that explain why the two sets of leaves were different after three days.

_____

_____

6. What other things do green plants need to produce food?

_____

7. Where do these things come from?

_____

_____

8. What would happen if the plant did not have these things? Can you think of a situation in which this might happen?

_____

_____

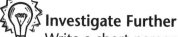

Investigate Further

Write a short paragraph about what you think would happen if sunlight were blocked by thick smoke or other air pollution for a very long time. Brainstorm ideas for your paragraph and then organize them before you begin writing.

• Investigate 2—*How Producers Reproduce* •

Most plants grow from a seed or from a part of the parent plant that was cut off and rooted in water or soil. The seed is the result of the male pollen fusing with the female ovule. Both the pollen and the ovule develop in the reproductive organ of many plants, the flower. The joining of the pollen (sperm) and ovule (egg) is called *sexual reproduction*. In the case of a rooted cutting, there is only one parent. This is called *asexual reproduction*. In this investigation, you will grow some new plants.

Materials
whole potato with eyes
lima bean seed cut into halves
lima bean seed soaked in water
    for 2 or more hours

pieces of potato with eyes
water
2 flowerpots or paper cups
    filled with soil

Procedure
1. Look for the eyes on the potato. Using a piece of potato provided by your teacher, draw the piece in the space provided.
2. Plant the potato piece in a flowerpot. Cover with soil and water.
3. Place the flowerpot in a sunny spot. Observe it daily.
4. Look at the lima bean seed. The large scar on the side is where the bean seed was attached to the pod. The tiny hole beneath it is where the pollen entered the ovule. Draw the bean seed in the space provided on page 78.
5. Look at the lima bean seed halves your teacher gives you. Draw the embryo (baby plant) that is inside.
6. Plant the remaining bean seed in a flowerpot. Water and place it in a sunny spot. Observe it daily.

Potato with Eyes

Potato Piece with Eyes

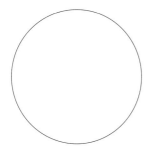

Bean Seed

Bean Seed with Embryo

Observations

1. Did a new potato plant grow? _____

2. Did a new bean plant grow? _____

3. Which plant resulted from sexual reproduction? _____

4. Which plant resulted from asexual reproduction? _____

5. In the spring, dandelion seeds are blown by the wind. If they land on moist soil, they will grow into new dandelion plants. Is this an example of sexual or asexual reproduction? Explain your answer.

_____

_____

_____

Investigate Further

Seeds are often found inside fruits. The fruit protects the seed and helps move it away from the parent plant. Near the parent, it would not be able to compete successfully for light and water. Animals eat the fruits. They later eliminate the seeds from their bodies far away from the parent plant.

Seeds develop in a part of the flower called the *ovary.* Find the ovary in the drawing. In many plants, the ovary develops into the fruit with the seeds inside. Some fruits are tomatoes, string beans, apples, oranges, and cucumbers. List the names of as many different kinds of fruit as you can.

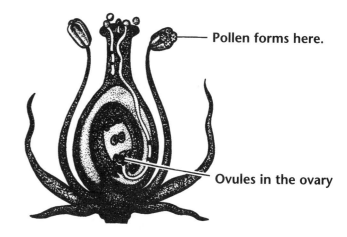

Pollen forms here.

Ovules in the ovary

**Sexual Reproduction
in Plants**

• Investigate 3—*Moving Molecules* •

The cell membrane that surrounds the cell controls which molecules move into the cell and which ones move out of the cell. The cell must use up some energy to get some necessary molecules in, but others move in on their own. These molecules diffuse into the cell through the cell membrane. *Diffusion* is the movement of molecules from an area where there are many of them to a place where there are only a few or none of them. In this investigation, although you cannot see molecules, you will see proof that diffusion happens.

Materials

4 beakers	hot and cold tap water
medicine dropper	food coloring
distilled water	5% salt solution
cubes of peeled potato	balance (optional)
paper towels	stopwatch or clock with a second hand

Caution: Do not drink the water or eat the potatoes used in this investigation.

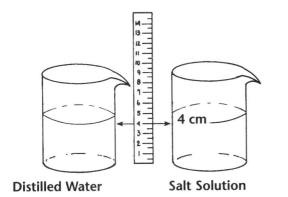

Distilled Water   **Salt Solution**

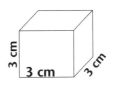

Potato Piece

Procedure

1. Fill one beaker almost to the top with hot water. Fill the other beaker with cold water. Let them sit for 2 minutes.
2. Gently drop 5 drops of food coloring into the hot water.
3. Watch the color move from the area where you put the drops to every part of the water. Time how long this movement takes.
4. Repeat this procedure with the beaker of cold water. Again, time the movement.
5. Pour distilled water to a height of 4 cm in one beaker. Pour the salt solution to a height of 4 cm in another beaker.

6. If you have a balance, weigh the cubes of potato that are to be placed in the distilled water. Record the weight in the data table below. Does the potato feel firm or soft? Record your observations. Place the cubes in the distilled water. Let the potato cubes remain in the liquid overnight.
7. Repeat Step 6, but place the cubes in the salt water.
8. Remove the cubes from the liquids. Blot them with paper towels.
9. Weigh the cubes that had been in the distilled water. Feel them. Record your observations in the data table.
10. Repeat the procedure with the cubes that had been in the salt water.

		Before Treatment	After Treatment
Distilled Water	Weight Feel (firm or soft)		
Salt Water	Weight Feel (firm or soft)		

Observations

1. What happened to the food coloring in the water?

_____

2. In which beaker was the diffusion faster?

_____

3. Why do you think this happened?

_____

4. What happened to the potato in the distilled water?

_____

5. What happened to the potato in the salt water?

_____

6. Look at the beaker that contained the potato cubes in distilled water. Do you think more water molecules were inside the potato cells or outside in the water?

_____

7. Which way would the water molecules move—into the cells or out from the cells? Remember the definition of diffusion.

_____

8. Does the information collected from your investigation show this to be true? Explain your answer.

_____

_____

9. Look at the beaker that contained the potato cubes in salt water. Do you think there were more water molecules inside the cells or outside in the salt water?

_____

10. Which way would the water molecules move—into the cells or out from the cells?

_____

11. Does the information collected from your investigation show this to be true? Explain your answer.

_____

_____

12. The diffusion of water across a cell membrane is called *osmosis*. Do you think the salt molecules diffused? Why?

_____

13. If the salt molecules did move into the cell, would you call that process osmosis? Explain your answer.

_____

_____

Investigate Further
Mix some cornstarch with water and pour it into a small plastic bag. Use thread to tie the bag so that none of the starch solution can leak out. Put the bag into a beaker half filled with water. Let it sit overnight. What happened? Can you explain it? Add three or four drops of iodine solution. What happened?

• Investigate 4—*Why Consumers Need Oxygen* •

To stay alive, the human body needs oxygen. The oxygen is needed to help burn or change the food in the cells. This taking in of oxygen and burning of food is called *respiration* and makes energy for the life functions. Respiration takes place all of the time. You breathe in oxygen even while you are asleep. The average breathing rate for humans is 16 to 20 breaths per minute.

Materials
stopwatch or clock or watch with a second hand

Caution: Obtain permission from your teacher before participating in any exercises.

Procedure
1. Choose a partner.
2. Sit quietly for 1 minute. Have your partner count your breathing rate for 1 minute by watching you inhale and exhale.
3. You keep track of the time. Tell your partner when to start and to stop counting.
4. Record this rate in the first data table below.
5. Exercise for 2 minutes by doing jumping jacks.
6. Immediately sit down and repeat Steps 2 and 3 ten times.
7. Record the results in the second data table below.
8. Plot a line graph of these results. Use the grid on page 83.

Normal Breathing Rate	Breaths per Minute
(after one-minute test)	

Minutes after Exercise	Breaths per Minute
1	
2	
3	
4	
5	
6	
7	
8	
9	
10	

Breathing Rate after Exercise

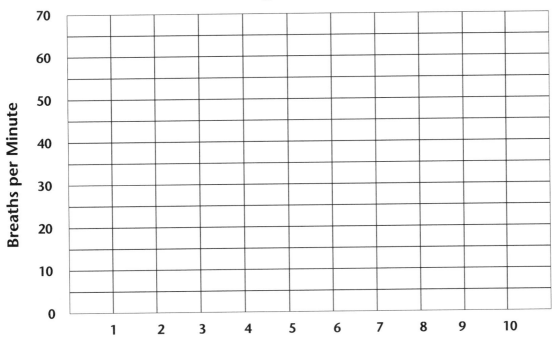

Time in Minutes

Observations

1. What was the effect of exercise on your breathing rate? _____

   _____

2. How many minutes passed before your breathing returned to normal? _____

3. Were your resting and maximum breathing rates the same as those of others
   in your class?

   _____

   _____

Investigate Further

Do some research and experimentation to compare the effects of age and
long-term exercise on breathing rates. Compare human breathing rates to
those of other animals such as horses, elephants, mice, and birds.

Food is the fuel that animals need to provide energy for living. It must be broken down into molecules before it can be used. Remember that a molecule is the smallest particle of a substance. The breaking down of food into usable molecules is called *digestion*. Digestion begins in the mouth where your teeth grind food into small pieces. Then the chemicals take over. The chemicals produced by your body to digest foods are called *enzymes*. Amylase is in your saliva. In this investigation, you will find out what amylase does.

Materials

unsalted crackers
iodine
metric ruler
water
Benedict's solution
test tube rack
beaker for water bath

paper towel
3 test tubes
crayon
amylase solution
test tube tongs
hot plate
oven mitts

3. cracker in amylase solution
2. amylase solution
1. cracker in water

Caution: Always use oven mitts when handling the hot plate and heated containers. Do not eat the crackers used in this investigation. Do not touch the iodine, amylase solution, or Benedict's solution.

Procedure

1. Place a cracker on a paper towel. Use a medicine dropper to put two drops of iodine on the cracker. The iodine will turn purple if starch is present in the cracker.
2. Fold the cracker up in the paper towel and throw it away.
3. Label the test tubes 1, 2, and 3.
4. Measure 1.5 cm from the bottom of the test tubes. Draw lines with the crayon.
5. Add water up to the line in test tube 1 and add amylase solution up to the line in test tubes 2 and 3.
6. Crush a cracker and put one-half of the crushed cracker in test tube 1 and the other half in test tube 3.
7. Put 12 drops of Benedict's solution into each test tube.
8. Place the three test tubes into a beaker of boiling water for three minutes. Observe and record your observations in the data table on page 85.

Tube	Contents	Color	Sugar Present?
1			
2			
3			

Note: Benedict's solution is normally blue. If it is heated gently, however, in the presence of simple sugar molecules, it will turn green and then yellow to orange. The more sugar molecules present, the greater the color change.

Observations

1. Was there starch in the cracker you tested with iodine? _____

2. Did test tube 1 have sugar in it? _____

3. Did test tube 2 have sugar in it? _____

4. Did test tube 3 have sugar in it? _____

5. If the answer to question 4 is yes, where did the sugar come from?

   _____

   _____

6. Amylase solution contains an enzyme like the enzyme in your saliva. What does your saliva help do? How?

   _____

   _____

   _____

Investigate Further

Research information about the digestive process in reference books and on the World Wide Web. Take notes summarizing the information. Write a brief report describing the digestive process and its importance. Begin by organizing your notes.

• Investigate 6—*You and Your Heart* •

The circulatory system of the human body is made of a pump (the heart) and a system of tubes called *veins, arteries,* and *capillaries.* The heart is a powerful muscle that never rests. The squeezing and relaxing of the heart muscle is known as the *heartbeat.* Our pulse is just a result of the blood pressure created by the heart. The circulatory system carries nutrition to the cells and moves waste away from the cells.

Materials

stopwatch or clock with a second hand

Caution: Obtain permission from your teacher before participating in any exercises.

Procedure

1. Locate your pulse as shown in the diagram.
2. Sit quietly for 2 minutes.
3. You keep track of your pulse by counting the beats.
4. Your partner will time you for one minute. He or she will tell you when to start and to stop.
5. Record this rate in the first data table.
6. Exercise for 2 minutes by doing jumping jacks.
7. Immediately sit down and repeat Steps 3 and 4 ten times.
8. Record the results in the second data table.
9. Plot a line graph of these results. Use the grid on page 87.

Normal Pulse Rate	Pulse Rate (beats per minute)
(after two-minute test)	

Minutes after Exercise	Pulse Rate
1	
2	
3	
4	
5	
6	
7	
8	
9	
10	

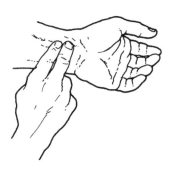

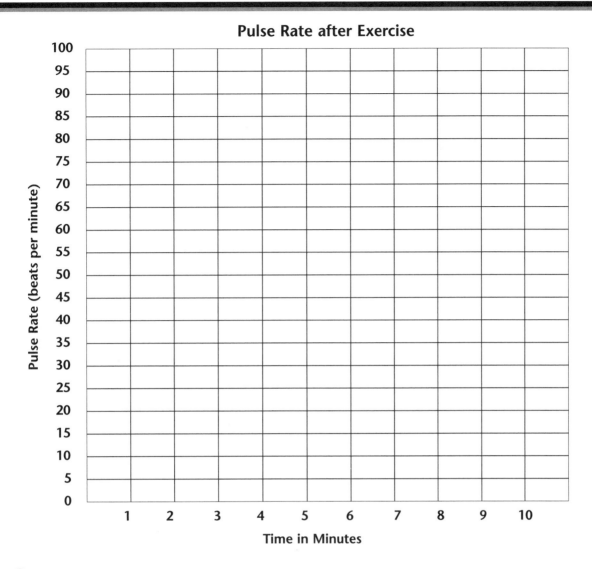

Pulse Rate after Exercise

Pulse Rate (beats per minute)

Time in Minutes

Observations

1. What was the effect of exercise on your pulse? _____

_____

2. How many minutes passed before your pulse rate returned to normal?_____

3. Were your resting and maximum pulse rates the same as those of your classmates?

   Explain. _____

_____

Investigate Further

Do some research and experimentation to compare the effect of age and long-term exercise on pulse rates. Also, compare human pulse rates to those of other animals such as horses, elephants, mice, and birds.

Many physical traits are caused by the presence of certain genes. *Genes* are bits of information in the nucleus of the cell. One-half of all of that information in the nucleus came from your mother. The other half came from your father. Some traits are caused by one *dominant gene*. A dominant gene controls the appearance of a certain characteristic or trait. If a dominant gene is not present, then another trait, called a *recessive trait*, will show up. For example, the dominant gene for eye color is brown. If a person inherits one brown gene, his or her eyes will be brown. A recessive gene for eye color is blue. If a person inherits one brown gene and one blue gene, his or her eyes will be brown. If a person inherits two blue genes—one from each parent—his or her eye color will be blue. In this investigation, you will look at some human genetic traits. You will find out if you have the trait and then figure out what genes you have for what trait.

Procedure

1. Determine which of each of the following traits you have. Answer each question.

   a. Are your earlobes
      unattached or attached?

      _____

   b. Is your little finger
      bent or straight?

      _____

   c. Do you have a straight
      thumb or a hitchhiker's
      thumb?

      _____

   d. Does your hairline have a widow's
      peak or is it straight?

      _____

   e. Are you able to roll your tongue?

      _____

2. Record your observations in the following data table.

Trait	Do You Have It?	Your Possible Genes

- Unattached ear lobes (A)   Attached ear lobes (a)
- Bent little finger (B)   Straight little finger (b)
- Straight thumb (H)   Hitchhiker's thumb (h)
- Tongue rolling (R)   No tongue rolling (r)
- Widow's peak (W)   Straight hairline (w)

An uppercase letter, which represents the gene, has been placed after each dominant trait. A lowercase letter, which represents the gene, has been placed after each recessive trait. Since everyone has two genes for each trait, you might have two dominant genes, one dominant gene and one recessive gene, or two recessive genes.

3. Draw ten squares and ten circles on a separate piece of paper. This will make two squares and two circles for each of the traits you are studying.

4. Mark one square with an uppercase letter. Mark one square with a lowercase letter. Do the same with the circles. Do this for each of the five traits you have looked at. See the following examples.

The squares represent the genes from one parent. If a person has unattached ear lobes, for example, he or she will have one or two A's. A person with two a's will have attached ear lobes. Let us see how this works.

5. A person with the dominant trait will have _____ or _____ genes.

6. A person with the recessive trait will have _____ genes only.

Cut out the shapes and use the squares and the circles to indicate your possible genes.

7. The following vocabulary words are useful in describing some of the things you have learned in this lesson.

Genotype	the letters used to indicate the genes that a person has for a certain trait; for example, **Aa**
Phenotype	the appearance of a person in terms of a certain trait; a person with **Aa** genotype has unattached ear lobes; this is his or her phenotype
Pure dominant	a genotype in which both genes are dominant
Hybrid	a genotype in which one gene is dominant and the other is recessive
Genetics	the study of inheritance

Observations

1. If you have the dominant trait, can you be sure about which letters you use? Explain your answer.

_____

_____

2. If you have the recessive trait, can you be sure about which letters you use? Explain your answer.

_____

_____

3. Record your possible genes in the data table on page 89.

4. Sometimes parents who both have the dominant trait have children who have the recessive characteristic. How could this happen? Use your cutout pieces to work this out. Make each parent **Aa**.

   a. If parent #1 contributes an **A** and parent #2 contributes an **A**, what genes will the child have? Will this be the dominant or the recessive trait?

   _____

   b. If parent #1 contributes an **A** and parent #2 contributes an **a**, what genes will the child have? Will this be the dominant or the recessive trait?

   _____

   c. If parent #1 contributes an **a** and parent #2 contributes an **a**, what genes will the child have? Will this be the dominant or the recessive trait?

   _____

5. Think about your answers to the last question. What do you think is meant when someone is called a *carrier?* For example, normal parents who have a child with sickle-cell anemia are carriers.

   _____

• Investigate 8—One Fossil per Hour •

It takes thousands of years for fossils to form. Fossils are the imprints or remains of living things. Most fossils that have been found were in sedimentary rocks. By studying fossils, it is possible to tell what kinds of organisms lived long ago and how they have changed over millions of years. In this investigation, you will make some "fossils" in just a few days. Although your models will take a short time, the fossil-making process is the same.

Materials

large container
plaster of paris
plastic margarine container
"fossil" material (leaf, dead bug, shell)

large spoon
water
petroleum jelly
food coloring

Procedure

1. Mix the plaster of paris and water according to directions in a large container. It should feel like thick mud.
2. Coat the inside of the margarine container with petroleum jelly. This allows for easy removal of the plaster cast.
3. Use a large spoon to fill the container with plaster of paris to a depth of 5 cm (2 inches).
4. Coat the "fossil" material with petroleum jelly. Firmly press it into the plaster.
5. Let the plaster harden overnight.
6. Remove the "fossil" material the next day. You should be able to see its imprint.
7. Coat the entire top of the plaster (including the imprint) with petroleum jelly.
8. Mix more plaster of paris. Add some food coloring to show a different layer of mud on top of the original layer.

9. Spoon this new layer on top of the old one. Allow it to harden.

10. After it has hardened, remove the "rock" from the container. Split the layers apart to reveal the "fossil."

Observations

1. Which layer of rock is the oldest, the white layer or the colored one?

_____

2. Suppose shark tooth fossils were in a rock known to be twenty million years old and fish scale fossils in the layer above it. Which animals were probably there first, the sharks or the fish?

_____

3. Compare your fossil to others made by your classmates. What kinds of material made the best fossils? Explain your answer.

_____

4. Why do you think few fossils of worms and jellyfish are found, but many fossils of snail shells and bones found?

_____

_____

_____

_____

5. Explain how fossils are formed.

_____

_____

_____

_____

_____

_____

• Investigate 9—*Cold Hands, Warm Heart* •

The human body is constantly changing. Your body tries to keep some things the same. When you are hungry, your body is trying to tell you to eat. When you exercise, your breathing and heart rates increase because your body needs more oxygen. What about your body temperature? When it is cold, your body works hard to keep warm. When it is hot, your body systems struggle to keep cool. How good of a job does your body do? In this investigation, you will study body temperature.

Materials
disposable thermometer or temperature strip

Caution: Do not reuse a thermometer. Dispose of the thermometer as instructed immediately after taking your temperature.

Procedure
1. Form groups of up to five boys and five girls.
2. Make a data table in which to record each group member's temperature.
3. Take your temperature using a disposable thermometer or temperature strip.
4. Record the results in the data table you made.
5. Make a bar graph of these results.

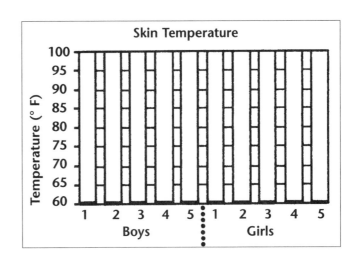

Observations
1. Was your temperature the same as everyone else's? _____

2. Was there any difference between boys' and girls' temperatures?

_____

_____

Investigate Further
Do some research and experimentation to compare the effect of age and body size on temperature.

Review Unit 4

Across Clues

3. The type of reproduction involving two parents.
4. A powerful pumping muscle of the circulatory system.
5. The sweet energy source that plants make.
6. The movement of molecules from an area of many like molecules to an area of a few.
8. Letters that can represent dominant and recessive genes.
9. Reproduction that involves only one parent.
12. The food-making process of plants.
13. The very old imprints or remains of living things.

Down Clues

1. A waste produced by plants that is important to animals.
2. The "burning" of food to produce energy.
7. The study of inheritance.
10. Chemicals that assist in digestion.
11. Chemical structures responsible for physical traits.

End-of-Book Test

A Use words from the box to complete each of these sentences.

sedimentary rock	plates	crust	mantle	core
metamorphic rock	luster	wind	minerals	igneous rock

1. The innermost layer of the earth is the _____.

2. Air in motion is called _____.

3. Melted rock that hardens is _____.

4. Pieces of earth's lithosphere are called _____.

5. The ability of a mineral to reflect light is called _____.

6. Rock formed by great pressure and heat is _____.

7. The earth's outer layer is its _____.

8. Solid substances formed naturally in the earth are _____.

9. Small pieces of rock "glued" together form _____.

10. The middle layer of the earth is called the_____.

B Write the letter of the best answer in the blank.

_____ 1. An ice cube is an example of a
        a. liquid.   **b.** solid.
        c. solution.   **d.** gas.

_____ 2. The smallest part of a compound is
        a. an element.   **b.** an atom.
        c. a molecule.   **d.** sodium.

_____ 3. An example that is a result of a chemical change to matter is
        a. torn paper.   **b.** broken glass.
        c. rust.   **d.** melted ice.

_____ 4. A magnet will attract
        a. steel.   **b.** paper.
        c. wood.   **d.** glass.

C Match each item in Column 2 to the appropriate item in Column 1.

Column 1

_____ 1. plant

_____ 2. animal

_____ 3. cell

_____ 4. pollutants

_____ 5. species

_____ 6. nucleus

_____ 7. seed

_____ 8. microorganisms

_____ 9. fungi

_____ 10. cotyledon

Column 2

a. mushrooms, molds, and yeast

b. the building block of organisms

c. smallest classification group of organisms

d. organism that produces its own food

e. bacteria and amoebas

f. materials that can be harmful to living things

g. human, snake, or fish

h. seed leaf of plant

i. the "brain," or control center, of a cell

j. next generation of a plant that contains an embryo

D Unscramble the letters in parentheses to spell the word that best completes each sentence. Write the unscrambled word in the blank.

1. (o s s p o t y h i n s t e h)

    The food-making process of plants is called _____.

2. (l o p e n l)

    In sexual reproduction in plants, _____ and an ovule join together.

3. (f u n d o i f i s)

    The movement of molecules from an area with many of them to an area with few

    of them is called _____.

4. (p o t s i r i n e r a)

    The process in which oxygen is used to burn food in the cells is called _____.

5. (t o n e s i g i d)

    The process in which food is broken down into molecules is called _____.

6. (m a i n t o n d)

    If a _____ gene is not present, a person will have a recessive trait.